Praise for 360

Hold on to your hat as you immerse yourself in this inspiring action packed story of adoption, abuse, relinquishment, secrets, and despair that eventually leads to dreams coming true. Carol Welsh has resolutely grappled with multiple hardships, while always reaching for her star. In the process she found healing and joy. Unable to put her book down once I started it, I believe there is nothing this remarkable woman could not achieve if she decided to go for it. And somehow she gives you the feeling that this can happen for you too. *Titia Ellis, PhD, author of The Search: a Memoir of an Adopted Woman*

What a great story. I loved it!! I just feel as if I know you so well. You are a remarkable woman with a courageous spirit. Isn't it funny how people who go through so many hardships in their life usually turn out to be the most interesting? And isn't it also funny about family lies and secrets? Some live with them and never question them. Some ache to tell the truth and, after a while, cannot hold it back any longer. You are a role model for those who want to live their true path. *Mary Gediman, author "Journeywoman"*

Everyone in this world seems to pathologize the adopted child (and Carol had her share of acting out), but there is not enough scrutiny toward the attachment issues of the adults and how they impact that child. Carol is a very sane (if not quirky!) woman even after loss, trauma, and more loss. It is astounding that she trusts anyone to this day and yet she does. *360 Square* is important reading for all professionals in the adoption field. *Dr. Joyce Maguire Pavao, Pre/Post Adoption Consulting and Training (PACT), Cambridge, MA and New York*

i

I found Carol's story to be compelling, sensitively written, and the fact all of it is true makes the book even more powerful.
*Judith Berry, Attorney who focuses her practice on adoption and surrogacy law*

*360 Square* has helped me in my practice as an adoption social worker in a way I never expected. The feeling Carol openly and generously shares throughout her journey has deepened my understanding of adoption being a life-long process. I would recommend this book to all members of the adoption triad. I couldn't put it down.
*Sue LoBosco, LCSW Clinical Supervisor*

A remarkable story: A remarkable person.
Here is an ordinary young person in heartbreaking circumstances looking for herself. But she is alone. There is no road map, no material or emotional support – no safety net of any kind – only grit, pluck, and a Dream Woman.
*Carol Rothenberg, Speech and Language Pathologist*

You'll feel so deeply for this woman, determined to learn her own life story. Carol's amazing journey will strap you into the passenger seat and you won't want to get off even after the final page is read. By the way, bring a hanky for the ride.
*Robert Strauss, Business Owner, Director Camp Wigwam*

I think you have done a wonderful job with this book, developing your amazing story gracefully and with suspense. The diverse characters are very well realized. I would say that "360" is now complete —as your life would seem to be.
*Sally Paynter, Freelance Editor and mother of two adopted children*

A rare voice that illustrates the conflicting feelings from the perspective of each member of the adoption triad: grief, joy, anger, courage and everything in between.
*Stephanie Mitchell, LICSW, Executive Director, Maine Adoption Placement Services*

# 360 Square

## A Memoir of Adoption
## and Identity

The names of several people, along with identifying
descriptions, have been changed to protect and respect
their privacy. I have also reconstructed various
conversations and condensed certain moments of my
life. As with all memoir, this is my perspective of my
experiences and everything is accurate to the best of my
recollection.

The 360 Square logo is a pending
Registered Trademark ® of
Carol Ann Enterprises, LLC

Cover design by Judith Paolini, tdpa.com

To contact Carol, visit
www.carol-welsh.com

LCCN: 2012906509
Library of Congress Cataloging-in-Publication Data
Pending

ISBN-13: 978-1475174670
ISBN-10: 1475174675

For my mothers, my families
and everyone
who is touched by adoption.

Tossed Out

July 1962 – Riverside, Connecticut

If my life were normal I'd have been lying on my stomach at the end of my bed, knees bent, feet in the air, wiggling my toes while talking on the phone with a girlfriend, or writing about a boyfriend in my diary. But not me—not Carol Ann McCallum.

Instead, bilious vomit burned the back of my throat while my stomach churned then heaved a last time as I knelt hunched over on all fours a street away from home, puking up my guts, with the dim light from the corner street lamp casting a bizarre dog-like silhouette of a sixteen-year-old girl on the ground before me.

Finally purged, salty tears mixed with slimy snot slid down my upper lip. Not giving a shit who saw me out of control, gasping, sobbing, I crawl-walked, monkeylike, to the nearest tree, leaned against it and unsuccessfully willed it to swallow me up, to take me into its limbs, to rock and comfort me for having been grabbed by the scruff of the neck and seat of my pants then thrown down the front steps of my house by my crazed father.

Arriving home ten minutes late from play-practice at the Congregational Church in Old Greenwich and finding the kitchen door locked knotted my gut.

The house was as dark as a black cat on a moonless night, the only light coming from a carriage lamp perched atop the lamppost by the kitchen entry.

Small hairs rose tall then danced on the back of my neck. Adrenaline coursed through my veins. Alerted intuition called for courage. Scanning the yard, I

1

scurried past graceful rose bushes and strong smelling tomato vines to the back door. Locked too! I could shimmy up the gutter pipe by my bedroom window (the usual sneaking-out route) but didn't want to tip my hand on that one.

So going 'round to the front I peered through my parents' bedroom window. Silhouettes backlit by the butter colored bathroom night-light stood talking to each other. I knocked on the window with increased force trying to get their attention; time expanded as they ignored me, and my gut roiled again. They were all inside together, my father, mother, and kid sister with the power to let me in but choosing not to because I was different, a black sheep, the bad one who didn't follow the rules (though I *was* more like my father than I would ever have cared to admit).

Dad never backed down, never surrendered; to surrender was shameful. Dad only ladled out shame; he didn't accept it. There I was mule-like, banging on windows because I wouldn't give up either.

Spying movement toward the front of the house, I expected to be let in.

Dad opened the door with force, stuck his graying, freckled head out before his pajama clad body and in the voice of Darth Vader said, "You're not welcome here any more."

Cutting through all my offered explanations and reasons, he reiterated that he had warned me breaking rules demonstrated disrespect for him. This was it. The final straw! He was done with me. I was no longer allowed in his house.

Preposterous, a bunch of bullshit to scare me into submission: a challenge. I continued to press my case and myself toward the open door. He stood firm bellowing about the rules.

Matching anger with anger I vented sixteen years' worth of venom by yelling, "I hate your stupid rules, your controlling rules, your craziness! You never listen.

2

You accuse me of lying when I'm telling the truth. You don't hear anything I say. You're always trying to control me!" We quickly digressed into angry nonsense. No longer talking but attacking. I'd had it; he'd had it. He was right; no, I was right. He was a control freak; I was a disobedient child, and nothing was worse in the world. "You bastard! You're *not* my father. I hate you! I hate you! I hate you!"

Face blood red, neck cords taut, eyes bulging way beyond the usual hairy eyeball stage, he grabbed me by the hair and shirt, jerked me off my feet, and threw me down the porch steps. "Bastard, you call me? *You're* the little bastard. In fact, you're nothing but a liar and a whore." Pointing his forefinger that tonight seemed the size of a kielbasa sausage at me with tiny knuckle hairs rippling he ordered, "Get out of my house for good," then backed into the house slamming and locking the door, before turning out the lights. The metallic pop of the deadbolt hitting home emphasized the finality of his actions and reverberated in my ears for days to come.

Defiantly, I brushed myself off, checked for bleeding where his silver ID bracelet had hit my temple, then stumbled down the street sobbing. Unsure of where I was going, I trudged along in the twilight, sniffling, unaware of the warm breeze that caressed my bare arms. Behind screened doors with fans running on high, people watched television, ate ice cream, laughed, and were a family; while I plodded alone, angry as a nor'easter, hating my father more and more as reality sunk in with each step.

Stupid asshole! Who appointed *him* God? Dumb shit-head! I'd show him! He wouldn't win this one!

3

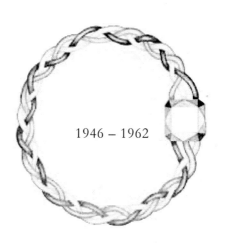

1946 – 1962

## Square Peg In A Round Hole

### 31 May 1946

Glenn and Margaret McCallum had taken extra time this morning to dress just right in order to maintain a good impression. They arrived an hour early in their joyfulness over picking up their baby girl from the Spence Chapin Adoption Agency in New York City. At six months I was adorable in spite of being bald—not shiny bald, just fuzzy bald. Mother insisted on attaching a pink bow to the top of my head with flour-and-water paste so she wouldn't have to hear how cute her little boy was, even though she'd dressed me head to toe in frilly pastel pink. By age two white-blonde hair and beautiful curly ringlets replaced the fuzz—that was until my first real haircut when those curls disappeared on the stylist's floor.

Wearing a stylish short brimmed hat, an ostrich feather sticking out of the left side, on her brown coiffed permanent-waved hair, head held high and posture perfect, Mommy pushed the baby carriage down the sidewalks of Larchmont with long-legged strides. People would see me sitting straight up, taking everything in while wearing a safety harness to keep me from leaping from the carriage should something exciting present itself for exploration.

Curious, yet shy and sensitive, I'd hide behind then peek out around Mother when meeting new people. With maturity and training I became socially poised and made friends easily. However, spontaneity and a vivid imagination coupled with great coordination got me into trouble early in life.

Mommy said I had a mind of my own right from the start, exerting my independence whenever given a chance. With pride she told anyone she could how advanced for my age she found me as compared to other children in the neighborhood and how very active and extremely curious a little person I was, with an inner sense of security and no fear.

She found pleasure in dressing me as her porcelain doll all in ruffles and lace with patent-leather shoes and white gloves. Margaret went to great lengths to buy beautiful clothes for me, even ordering from as far away as Europe. She expected me to sit daintily in those smocked dresses hosting tea parties with miniature china cups holding tiny handles that I pinched between thumb and forefinger, my pinky extended properly like the grownups, or playing carefully with paper dolls repeatedly changing their clothes. It didn't impress Mommy at all when, in a temper-tantrum of frustration or impatience, I'd tear the tags off the dolls' clothing or throw a teacup on the floor shattering it into tiny pieces.

Behind our townhouse the ground sloped upward seeming mountainous to a small child. At the summit stood a stately oak on whose long reaching arm Daddy installed a wooden swing where Skippy O'Rourke and I spent days pushing one another. If we weren't swinging we were digging in dirt piles nearby or climbing smaller maple trees and scaring Mom half to death by hanging upside down yelling, "Look at me!"

Below and to the left of our home were ball fields where Daddy would take me to practice throwing and catching. Anything athletic kept my interest. My knees usually sported a bump or bruise, hands were sticky with pine pitch and clothes often became dirty or grass stained much to Mother's dismay.

Still, Mom and Dad were as proud of my childhood accomplishments as they were frustrated by my independence. Valuing life experience they were willing to let me find my own way until I crossed an imaginary line arbitrated by them. If I stayed within those parameters they were there with open arms and a hug to welcome or comfort as needed. But if I wandered too far afield they felt it their duty to teach me a lesson either by punishing or spanking. Mother had been raised in a house with a parlor and felt our living room was meant for everyone's use but couldn't be enjoyed if not kept just right, so I was trained not to touch, climb on, or move things in this special space. If I didn't obey a swift smack on the bottom followed.

On outings to the Bronx Zoo, Nan – who was a year younger than me (and would be a lifetime friend) – and her mother Moo (short for Muriel) would sometimes go with us. Viewing the monkeys and chimpanzees, Mom would insist that monkey blood coursed through my veins. "Listen, that one's saying, 'Hi, Cousin Carol' and hanging upside down just like you do," which would bring giggles from all of us. Every month or so, our families would get together for dinner, either at their house in Mamaroneck or our townhouse in Larchmont. "Uncle Ivan" was the best ice cream maker I knew. And, he always let Nan and me lick the paddle.

A week or two every summer, Mom and Dad would drop me off at Dad's parents' cottage in Lake George, New York leaving me with my grandparents while they went off on a vacation of their own. I loved those summer days, spoiled by grandparents—the spoiling that is a grandparent's right and one of the most important reasons for being on this earth.

Grandfather McCallum was a guild carpenter who enjoyed having me hang out in his woodworking shop. Even though I was quite young, he'd foster my independence encouraging me to pound nails and pull-push a small keyhole saw for myself.

"GranPop, can we go now, please?" I would plead tugging on his calloused, thin hand, anxious to start our daily soon after sunrise morning walk down the long dirt driveway with mica sparkling like fairy's mirrors in the sunshine. Our destination was the spring, each of us carrying silver galvanized pails for our day's drinking water. On the way back GranPop'd carry both pails so I could pick handfuls of tiny-blossomed forget-me-nots to give to GranMum. Good-naturedly she'd always find another jelly jar and another spot to put them until they turned brown and died. The small cabin turned blue with forget-me-nots when I visited.

GranMum's Scottish accent was so thick that my little ears sometimes couldn't distinguish what she was saying. To her I wasn't a girl but a gettle. She'd say to her husband, "Dad, take the gettle to the gartn and get me soome herbs for the scrumbled eggs this marnin, will ya."

Every two or three days GranPop would set a washtub out on a big whale-shaped rock he'd painted to resemble a shark. There it would sit until mid-afternoon when the sun's warmth had heated the water. Sitting in the beautifully crafted wooden chair her husband had made for her beneath a big gnarly, grey-barked apple tree, GranMum would peel bright red fruit that she'd later press into homemade applesauce that tasted sweet and tart at the same time, while I splashed in the No. 10 galvanized tub squealing with delight. GranMum would chat away in her Scottish brogue while nearby GranPop whistled, hoeing in the garden and stopping occasionally to acknowledge her.

Their field gradually increased in elevation rising away from the house until it abruptly ran into tall evergreens and conifers that continued all the way to the tip of the mountain. Between the upslope edge of the garden where he grew potatoes and the stately line of hunter green cone shaped silhouettes, stood the barn, a grey weathered structure that leaned slightly uphill looking like a skier does when standing sideways on a trail, their downhill leg long and straight, ski-edge tipped into the snow for maximum stability. As I entered the coolness of the barn, light peeked through the warped lopsidedness and earthy dry dirt and long gone cow odor met my nostrils. Tools, garden equipment, and an old tractor that ran when it felt like it, paled next to the shiny black-cherry Pierce Arrow that, after me, was GranPop's pride and joy. Sometimes on rainy days when I grew tired of playing in the house he'd take me to the barn and sit me on his lap in the driver's seat. He'd tell me to steer left, then right, and straight on as he storied me on a road trip through the Scoott-ish High-lnds filled with his memories of hills gowned in purple heather.

At night I slept on a window seat in the main room that GranMum made into a bed from several painstakingly hand-quilted covers. A small potbellied stove nearby took the chill off the cabin with that wonderful warmth and smoky smell only wood provides. Each night GranMum and GranPop would sit on either side of me telling a made-up today story, or one from the old country, until I drifted off to sleep.

Early in 1948 Dad and Mom bought a piece of property in Riverside, Connecticut. Dad then spent all his free time building us a small two bedroom, single story, Cape-style house that he painted white. Sundays Mom and I would drive up to the property taking a picnic lunch with us for Daddy. My parents would walk through the stick walls and doorways discussing where the furniture would go and which room would be what while I collected silver knockouts from electrical boxes pretending they were real money. It took Daddy all summer and most of the fall to build our house. Just before gusty November winds blew the last brown leaves clinging to gray branches, we moved from Larchmont. Our house was one of seven or eight differently designed houses that lined each side of the street.

Beyond the fieldstone wall in our new back yard was a large flat field with a big farmhouse and a few trees, but none had good enough swing-arms. Dad promised he'd build me a fancy swing set, with a slide and climbing bar in the spring. Come winter I delighted in the squeak-scrunch-crunch sound of crisp snow under boots. Playing in the yard I rolled snow into balls till they were almost too big to handle, and then I'd grunt and groan while hefting them onto each other into a snowman. Lying next to the round white man with the carrot nose I'd make several snow angels to keep him company for the night. Not far from the house was an old farm with the perfect sledding hill. Weekends Daddy would pull me over to the farm on a sled then send me down the hill. Speed sent thrills all through me, like a good shiver. As the sled gained speed going faster and faster I'd gleefully squeal pig-like down the slope only to climb back up and do it again and again until my little legs could trudge no more.

Fall 1950

A caseworker from the Spence Chapin Agency had visited our house in the spring and now returned again. I was to become a big sister.

My parents told me an age-appropriate version of my own adoption story. I don't remember making a big deal out of it or feeling any different, instead simply accepting it for what it was and getting on with being a kid. At four, I didn't question where babies came from. It seemed normal that they might come from a store, just like groceries and pets.

I had a hard time sitting still while riding in the front seat between my parents the day we went to get my sister. Normally Dad would have made me move to the back and stop rooching around but my behavior was overlooked in their excitement at having another child.

"What are we going to name her?" I asked.

Smiling at me, Dad responded, "Ginny. Do you like that?"

Oval-faced Ginny smelled like baby-powder and formula. She rode on Mom's lap (no car seats in those days) while I touched her soft head and cheeks. My funny faces made her gurgle, oooh, and smile back at me.

Having a baby sister was fun, except when she was crying. Being the 'big sister' Mom would let me help change her diaper or feed her a bottle. It was my job to play with her in the afternoon while Mom prepared dinner.

Her pink and white crib sat adjacent to my bed with its periwinkle blue spread. At bedtime, dim light sneaking under our door, I'd listen for the soft seesaw of Ginny's breathing and match mine to hers before drifting off to sleep. In the morning she'd peer at me through crib slats, her big blue eyes watching intently, and giggle as I stuck out my tongue wagging it side to side.

Grandma and Grandpa Russell bought an already-built house in the same town a few streets over from us and moved to Connecticut soon after we got Ginny. I was particularly fond of the cuddly old man with soft hands and smooth skin who took me fishing, on nature walks in the woods, and played with *me* while everyone else fussed over Sister. Once or twice a month we ate Sunday dinner at their house, a classic nuclear family ritual. Dad and Grandpa would talk in the parlor (which really was a living room but my grandparents were old-fashioned and found it difficult to give up old familiarities) while Mom and Grandma prepared the meal in the kitchen. As far back as I remember, it was my task to help set the table. Flashing her wide, almost ear to ear toothy grin, Mom would patiently put her long fingers over mine as we placed the fork, knife, and spoon in its properly assigned location on the table.

13

Grandmother Russell wore her long grey hair pulled so tight in a bun that it acted like a facelift pulling her wrinkles toward the hairline. Her make-up was always applied just so, two round rouged circles on each cheek. Shopping only in New York at Lord and Taylor or Bonwit's, she presented a classily dressed figure even if in a housecoat. Shorter in stature than my mother by eight inches I didn't feel towered over by her. Grandma derived pleasure from teaching me household duties. Putting a soft cloth in my pudgy hand she'd show me how to dip into the jar of grey metallic-smelling paste and then, copying her short round strokes, we would polish the silverware that was so special it even had a name, Flanders. One could find her demonstrating the proper way to cut up vegetables for a yummy soup then trusting me with a knife, watching closely as I carefully mimicked her movements. She taught me to decipher weeds from flowers by crushing their leaves then smelling and licking my fingers. Sundays were fun and something I looked forward to, learning a whole host of skills over the years.

Early childhood adventures fueled my internal fire. Being with Daddy was great fun too. I liked helping him with yard work, picking up sticks while he raked in the spring, poking holes in dirt for seedlings which became plump juicy tomatoes in summer, or jumping in piles of crinkly, musty smelling leaves come fall. One of my favorite things to do with Daddy was developing photos in the basement darkroom—it was so exciting when the red bulb turned the world monochrome. Standing next to each other, the faint smell of cigarette smoke from his shirt tickling my nose, we'd wait for the image to magically appear on the paper floating on its back in developer.

Daddy loved to take moving pictures of me with his favorite toy, an eight-millimeter camera, while I played in the yard or at the beach. He'd show home movies in our basement where, using a sheet suspended on the painted concrete block wall as a makeshift screen, he set up a theatre with chairs in rows just like a real theatre. I'd watch patiently until the end of the reel and then beg him to run it backward so we could all laugh as I did things in reverse at high speed looking like a tiny Charlie Chaplin or one of the Three Stooges.

Summer meant the beach and playing in the ocean. "You love the water so much you must have fish for relatives," Mother would say. Standing on the shore with a giant multicolored beach towel in hand motioning for me to come out she'd holler, "Get out right now. Go build a sand castle. Look at you. You look like an alien you're so purple," shaking her head side to side.

I not only loved playing in water but just being outside in nature. You could usually find me there in sunshine or rain exploring, getting dirty, and often pretending to be different animals.

I couldn't wait to start kindergarten. Mrs. Trecarten made everything a thrilling adventure. Excitement over making friends, learning new things, and climbing on the jungle gym filled my days as I settled into the new routine.

I was a good student excelling in everything but math which I found challenging, much to Mom's consternation. In first grade Mrs. Lee sent a note home asking my parents for their help. We were studying money and I just couldn't grasp the concept.

Placing ten pennies on the table in front of me Mom said, "Count them."

"One, two, three, four...ten."

She took five away and placed a nickel on the table. "This is the same as the five pennies."

"No it's not. They are brown, and there are five of them, this is silver and there's only one." After two days of explanations, a parent-teacher conference, a trip to the grocery store to watch the cashier make change, and much frustration for everyone, I finally got it.

15

We were one of the first families on the street to own a television and probably because of the novelty of the thing I was allowed to watch one or two shows a day. One day while watching *The Rootie Kazootie Club* I called out, "Look Mommy, you have polka dots just like Rootie Kazootie's girl friend." Oops! Social faux pas extraordinaire!

"Carol. That's rude. These are called moles. Go sit on the chair in the hall right now and stay there till your father comes home."

Glad I didn't say her bucked teeth made her look like Roy Rogers' horse, Trigger.

If Margaret hadn't paid such close attention to her appearance, dressing well, putting on her face each day, she would have been unattractively plain. But Glenn's money bought expensive clothes, permed hair, make-up, and bright red lipstick that amazingly softened rather than accentuated her mouth that never closed completely because of those protruding upper teeth.

As Ginny grew, we became playmates with me being the protective big sister watching out for her. We were like most siblings: sisters first, friends second. I loved her with all my heart, although sometimes she was a little pain in the ass when she got into my things, and her worst fault was being a tattletale.

Both Mom and Dad enjoyed traveling and fortunately included my sister and me on many of their trips. Each fall we took a two-family vacation to Cape Cod with Nan and her parents. Nan and I loved to explore the beach, tormenting horseshoe crabs, collecting shells, and bodysurfing the swells while trying not to swallow the whole ocean or fill our bathing suit bottoms with sand.

Usually in late spring we'd go to Bonnie Oaks Resort in Vermont where I got to ride a real full-sized brown horse named Caisson and play with other vacationing children while our parents did adult activities.

One late September we went to The Egremont Inn in Massachusetts with "Uncle Walter and Aunt Gusta." There, I was allowed special privileges like staying up late as Dad waltzed me around the uneven wooden floor on his shoes to a live band. I followed his every step, not missing a beat, daydreaming I was one of the professional dancers on television. A smooth dancer himself, Dad thought he'd taught me well. When he proudly commented, "You'll be a good dancer some day, Carol," I swelled with pride, feeling taller and more grownup.

Mother spent less and less time with me, as she kept busy with Ginny, housework, and her garden and bridge clubs. But several times a year, just the two of us would take a day excursion by train into New York City for shopping at Macy's, Bonwit Teller, and my favorite store F.A.O. Schwarz where my eyes were inevitably bigger than my parent's pocketbook.

For my seventh birthday we went shopping, then met Dad for lunch at a Horn & Hardart automat (now Burger King). Quarters made a chu-klink noise as they dropped into a slot in the machine with little glass doors. I pushed a button and whirr-hmmmmm, out came hot food. After our meal, ice-skating and a show at Rockefeller Center completed the day. Mesmerized, I imagined one day becoming a Rockette—not something my parents aspired for me, although they had enrolled me in dance class at school.

Twice a month Mom would fasten a starched horsehair crinoline around my waist before I wriggled into a fancy party dress. After fixing my hair, buffing the Mary Janes, and stuffing my hands into white gloves, she'd drive me to the elementary school. There the girls lined up on one side of the gym, boys on the other. When Mrs. Peabody pressed the little metal gizmo concealed in her white-gloved hand, it made a clicking sound and the boys crossed the room in fast-forward vying to dance with a girl they liked best, but sometimes

17

having to settle for whoever was left over if they weren't fast enough. Once we all had partners the music started and off we'd whirl and twirl around the gym stepping on each other's toes, accusing one another of being stupid. Sometimes there weren't enough boys to go around and a few of the less-best liked girls had to sit out a dance (no girl-with-girl dancing in those days). When that happened to me a hollow sadness grew in my stomach, fostering feelings of rejection. I always tried to be one of the best-liked girls.

I didn't dwell long on or give a lot of thought to adoption; I simply accepted it as a fact of life. But, as I progressed through elementary school and exerted more fiery independence, things began to change and I found myself in trouble with my parents more often. Little things became big things. Taking some change off Dad's dresser, I sneaked over to the corner store for penny candy. Naturally I got caught. To teach me a lesson he forced me to write "I am a thief" fifty times on a piece of paper then tie it on a string around my neck wearing it the rest of the day, even when he insisted I accompany him to the hardware store. After this incident tension simmered beneath the surface between us while defiance became my M.O. and the fact that I was adopted came into my mind more frequently.

Dad's usual method of discipline was spanking. The problem—the older I got, the heavier-handed he got. Frequently using his belt for emphasis, he'd leave welts on my legs, buttocks, and back. Or he'd backhand me across the face leaving a red mark where the gold ring he wore on his right pinky finger had made contact.

By the end of third grade I'd received many lashings. I remember once when roughly dragging me into the bedroom I shared with my sister, Dad forced me over the end of the bed, held me in place with a knobby knee in my back and repeatedly swung his belt across my butt. I don't recall the catalyst for that particular lashing but I'm sure it was something that would have been minor in other families. With each snap of leather I shouted, "I hate you!" It became a duel. An inner stubborn force egged me on—louder and louder. "I hate you! I hate you! I hate you!" Painful searing heat rose on my skin but I continued yelling until I collapsed in wracking sobs, finally succumbing.

The pressure on my back eased, then the door slammed with such a loud whack I thought it had surely pulled out of its hinges.

Eventually mother came in and applied cool compresses to my wounds, tucked me into bed, and softly closed the door, leaving me to my own misery.

I dreamed…

*Dressed in a beautiful Cinderella-like white gown, a silky periwinkle lacy comforter over me, I'm lying on my big fluffy bed in the middle of a brightly colored field of wildflowers. Warm bare skin prickles from a sunny breeze and I smile at the sensation. Suddenly a shadow blocks the sun: father looms over me—a giant. He tosses a handful of periwinkle petals in the air and as they gently float down onto me, he piles heavy, flat stones on top, their weight forcing me deeper into the soft mattress. Sharp metal beneath pokes my spine. Searing pain knifes into my chest. I open my mouth to scream but nothing comes out. I can't breathe. Stone after stone flattens my body—until I am nothing.*

The next morning, the welts on my buttocks and thighs were so angry and raised I couldn't sit down. Dear mother scribbled a note to the teacher instructing her to have me stand at the back of the class. A lesson needed to be taught. The teacher went along with the humiliation, angering me even more.

Some dreams are like one-night stands flitting through one's consciousness; others take up residence.

19

This stone-blanket nightmare would have a long-term lease, and although I eventually stopped screaming out loud, it was a long time before I stopped waking up chilled, in bedding soaked with sweat.

Mother ran hot and cold. She stood up for me the day I acted out toward a girl who'd been making fun of me at school. Janice tormented me almost every day by calling me names or waiting till school got out to circle me on her bike as I walked home, coming dangerously close at times as if she was a fighter pilot strafing the enemy. Fed up, I impulsively shoved a stick between the spokes of the front wheel sending her onto the handlebars, fortunately hurting pride more than her body. Feeling proud of myself and powerful yet fearing the consequences, I ran home and relayed the details to Mom. Putting an arm around me, she listened patiently then stood up and walked purposefully to the wall phone. Running her left forefinger down the list of neatly typed numbers hanging on the wall by the device, she stuck a bony right forefinger into the round black holes and dialed. She held the receiver away from her head so I heard the swish, tic, tic, tic, swish, tic, swish, tic, tic... followed by brinnggg, brinnggg, then "Hello, June, this is Margaret. I'm calling to tell you to keep your daughter away from mine... No! She deserved what she got." *Yeah, Mom!*

But another time I'd been in the playground at the elementary school playing on the seesaw with a friend when the friend got off while I was up rather than waiting until we were level. Coming down quickly and grabbing the seat for balance, I almost severed my left pinky finger. Stuffing the badly mangled, bloody digit into my mouth I ran home to Mom crying, more scared than in pain.

Turning white as a ghost when she saw it she quickly leaned against the wall for support. As color returned to her face she told me to, "Stick it back in your mouth and go to bed."

20

I vaguely remember her wrapping it and giving me something like aspirin then saying, "Your father will be home in a few hours and he'll know what to do." The surgeon said I would have lost the finger if they had waited much longer. *Yeah, Mom!* Over the next couple of years, Dad became almost mad in his need to intimidate me. His punishments always involved great humiliation.

One spring trip to Cape Cod was particularly painful. Somewhere after crossing the Massachusetts border I announced, "I have to go to the bathroom." Dad told me to hold it for a bit. Thirty miles down the road feeling as if I would burst, I asked again, "Can we please stop?"

"I'll stop at the next gas station."

Desperately searching ahead for the next one I squeezed my buttock cheeks together so tightly I gained an inch in height. No gas stations. I tried distracting myself by looking for faces and animals in the clouds. Flying pigs, masked cats, and old men passed me by but no down-to-earth gas stations. "I can pee on the side of the road Daddy, pleeeaaase stop."

"No. We'll find one soon," he replied in that stubborn tone of his that meant we were on his terms.

Warm, wet urine seeped through my clothes saturating the cloth seat below in spite of the ironclad grip I held on my urethra, while tears slid down my face and a whimper escaped my lips.

"What now!" he hollered.

"I couldn't hold it!" I sobbed.

When we arrived at our rental cabin almost an hour later he dragged me out of the car, stripped my panties off and planted me bare bottomed on the hot-air furnace grate with the wet underpants in front of me. He instructed me to think about how disrespectful I'd been of him and his car as urine fumes drifted up my nose for emphasis.

If I didn't sit up straight enough at the dining table properly squaring my meal, he'd grab my plate with one hand, my arm with the other, then drag me into the kitchen and toss the food onto the floor. With a heavy hand he'd push me onto my hands and knees. "You don't deserve to eat at the table. You can eat off the floor tonight like a dog," he'd say, retreating through the swinging door between the kitchen and dining room that squeaked in sympathy.

I hate you! Who would serve a kid curried meat that looked like diarrhea and mushy green peas? I hated peas! They were cooked to an olive green, not like the fresh bright green ones I picked in GranPop's garden. *Yuck!*

Flicking the peas under the fridge, as if playing miniature pool, I felt confident knowing they would dry into hard little green balls, but what do I do with the brown stuff? *Maybe, shove it under the stove.*

Should I be caught in a lie (even one my sister falsely blamed on me), Dad would physically place me on a chair in our entryway facing the wall then make a point of walking past me multiple times repeating, "There's the liar," while shaking a bratwurst sized finger at me.

I wanted to stick my tongue out at him but knew better. Instead I stared at the ugly wallpaper. Stupid pattern didn't go anywhere. Not like me! As soon as I was old enough I was gonna run away. Run where the wind would take me like a leaf on a fall day.

At eight-and-a-half, I was assigned the disciplinary menial Saturday job of picking gravel out of the lawn, stone by stone. Humiliated, I refused to acknowledge my friends who watched and waited before finally giving up on me. Meanwhile, cute little Ginny, braided pigtails tied at the ends with bows to match her smocked dress and an apron that, of course, matched Mom's, was having fun licking cookie batter.

A very athletically fit man, Father towered over me at six foot one and, although in a conflict an angered parent should be more disciplined, he wasn't. Were his beatings enough to cause serious injury? No. Usually he'd grab the belt buckle with his dominant right hand whip it out of the belt loops and deliberately snap it against me as if it were a wet towel leaving red, raised, pointed welts that took days to heal. I remember clearly an incident when he'd said something derogatory about me at the dinner table and I'd emphasized my dissatisfaction by stupidly sticking my tongue out at him. He grabbed a steak knife and threatened to skewer me. Sliding off the dining room chair, I ran into the living room, ducked behind the blue upholstered Queen Anne chair, and made myself small by tucking into a ball pressing my bottom against the celery green wall successfully dodging the slice. From my safe place, not wanting him to win this time, I sang out, "Na-na-nahna-na. You missed me." A risky move and one I luckily got away with that time.

All these beatings and encounters never required medical attention, and fortunately didn't leave permanent scars, except on my psyche.

Fall of 1954

When GranPop McCallum died, I remember everyone being quiet as church mice, like there was a pregnant silence in the house, and Dad having red eyes for a long time. For several nights before falling asleep I cried, feeling effects of the tension in the house. But mostly I cried because I would miss going to the cabin that next summer as GranMum planned to sell the place and move to St. Petersburg, Florida where it was warmer and not so hard on an old woman. After she moved, she was good about writing letters asking me about school activities and who I liked best on Dick Clark's *American Bandstand* or *The Ed Sullivan Show* but I never saw her again.

CAROL LILLIEQVIST WELSH

The next spring, Dad raised the roof on the back of our house turning the attic into two bedrooms and a bath: one for me, the other for Ginny. (I believe he inherited some money when his mother passed.)

Now in the privacy of my own room with my parents downstairs, I hoped my life would improve and the stone blanket dream would cease. But still the nightmare persisted, allowing a more constant, deeper disrespect for my father to develop and conflicting with my natural love for him.

Mother became an Emily Post judge of me and focused her affection toward my better-behaved younger sister. Now she either took special notice or ignored me completely, depending on her mood. A distance grew between us, with her looking for things I did wrong rather than praising my virtues and accomplishments. She became less involved in my daily life and became an inspector, silently making lists of what she viewed as amiss or not proper. *Silently, that was the key word.*

Reprimands weren't just: "You wait till your father comes home." She was subtle, sneakier, more disengaged, more like a prison snitch you barely noticed watching for your most damning actions, then scribbling them down on paper to hand to the warden.

Coming home from school one day I grabbed the last pickle from the jar and absentmindedly put the empty jar back in the refrigerator. Of course Mother noticed. But did she say a word to me about it? No, she simply waited until my father came home and reported me, leaving him to mete out my punishment. She couldn't even confront me rationally and directly on something as minor as a pickle.

Conducting weekly white-glove inspections of our bedrooms, she would inevitably find the one elusive dust bunny clinging to the underside of my mattress despite the careful mopping I gave twice a week, trying hard to conform and please.

Life at home got progressively worse as I entered junior high school (seventh grade). *What made me so defiant, so out there, so too much to handle?* I didn't intentionally devise ways to piss off my parents. I just did stuff in my own way which was unfortunately mostly against the rules. Did being adopted influence me? Parts of me wanted to be a good daughter and follow the rules, do what it took to please them; while the impulsive, spontaneous and curious side of me damned the consequences and didn't even consider them. Was that any different from a biological child?

For a few years, my parents hoped 'away' summer camp would reform me and I welcomed the experience as well as the respite from the microscope. I lived in a rustic screen windowed cabin with other girls and learned new skills such as sailing, archery, and riflery. I proudly achieved the highest level–sharpshooter–which I hoped would surely make Dad proud of me. He'd been in the Army so had carried a gun.

Unfortunately, here too I came up short, breaking camp rules by smoking. Believe it or not it wasn't even my idea, but getting caught was a big deal. The director made an example of me and the other girl even though I begged him for mercy, on my knees like a criminal, knowing the consequences would have much larger ramifications than he could imagine.

There would be no break. "Hi Glenn, this is Frank up at Camp Takodah. I'm afraid you're gonna have to come up here tomorrow and pick Carol up. She's been smoking and we can't allow her to stay at camp."

I'd crossed the line again. *Shit!*

Riverside, Connecticut was a posh upscale suburb of New York City, the sort of place in which every postwar American family wanted to raise their kids— particularly the nouveau riche, those with first-or-second-generation money still in mid-climb up the U.S. socioeconomic ladder. Most men commuted to the City every day by train while we, their lily-white trophy families, stayed behind in the Eisenhower-era picture-postcard town behind white picket fences, manicured lawns, and pretty flowerbeds with friendly neighbors living *Leave It to Beaver* and *Dick Van Dyke Show* lives.

Margaret would stand at the kitchen sink finishing dinner's preparations and watch for Glenn to come into view as he walked home from the train station. Keeping an eye on the stove clock, at six-ten she'd remove yellow gloves and her apron to change into a nicer dress for dinner. She'd apply a fresh 'face', put on earrings and matching brooch that had been hand picked for her by Glenn from Yards, then check her perfectly filed and buffed fingernails before returning to the kitchen to mix the ritual Manhattan cocktail. As she took Dad's hat and coat she'd hand him his drink. They would exchange a peck-on-the-cheek kiss then move to the living room to sip their cocktails and listen to what went on in one another's day. We were living in a black-and-white world.

Black and white, right and wrong, there was no gray whatsoever in *my* house. My father wasn't any Ward Cleaver!

No in-between existed in our home. Father was white and right. Most always I was wrong. And so a nasty nimbus cloud shadowed my every step.

Ginny on the other hand never made mistakes. Did I detect some gloating on her part? He barked, she obeyed, end of story. If our life was like the perfect family portrait, I was the rascal in the back row making devil's horns behind everyone else's heads: a free spirit, nothing more. Demure, well behaved, always clean, Ginny was as innocent-looking as Bo Peep, as sweet as Norman Rockwell's *Mother's Little Angel*. A goody-goody! More wild and precocious, I epitomized a combination of Annie Oakley and Annette Funicello. In spite of liking my sister and having fun with her most of the time, I became a cautious sibling.

Was it just my sister's nature to be good? Perhaps she was more malleable in our father's hands? Or maybe she was just plain terrified of receiving the same treatment as I?

She conformed. I riled the beast.

CAROL LILLIEQVIST WELSH

Trouble in Peyton Place

This era was a time when being a strong father was what was most respected in a man. A man had to be married, have a family, and provide for them. Anything less and people would talk, creating wild accusations only spoken about in whispers. A misbehaving child was not to be coddled, queried, and understood, but instead punished and made an example of. Spare the rod and spoil the child—that was what a father was expected to do.

Dad played the role; that he played it more unreasonably than others was my bad luck. Still our community forgave him, or at least turned a blind eye to what was going on. There was no handbook on raising children then, no guidance available to men on the nuances of being a father, only the postwar military outlook on everything. Margaret may have read Dr. Benjamin Spock's *Baby and Child Care* during my baby and toddler years but there wasn't anything for men (or women) to refer to in raising their adopted teenage children. Glenn came from a generation when most men had worn the uniform, been screamed at by a sergeant, been made fools of for something (or nothing), and forced to peel potatoes or scrub bathroom floors "like a good soldier." That was how most men then raised their children. And just as there were differences between sergeants, some fathers were more reasonable than others, some more sadistic. My father leaned more toward the latter.

My safe haven was at the neighbors' houses. I arranged as many babysitting jobs as possible. Playing with kids still held my interest at eleven and twelve;

boys weren't constantly on my mind yet; if earning money, I was deemed worthy in my father's eyes as well as my own.

Several of our neighbors hired me. Mostly I worked for the Richardsons, acquaintances of my parents primarily through the neighborhood bridge club. Carolyn Richardson had a difficult time with her pregnancy and was still quite ill when she and the baby came home from hospital. Being their number-one sitter afforded me the luxury of spending a lot of time at their house helping Carolyn with household chores along with caring for new little Harry. I was both grateful for the money and respite from father's wrath and mother's snooping eyes.

Clothing and appearance became even more an issue with Mom and Dad being overly class and dress conscious. So far I'd managed to avoid the girly-girl wear of mother's dreams by convincing her how impractical they were, but we now clashed over what was appropriate for a teen to be publicly seen in. Our compromise was preppy—Connecticut preppy. This suited my athletic tomboy mode but did nothing for a clear desire to be attractive to boys. Mom forced me to wear shirtwaist dresses or poodle skirts, monogrammed button-down Oxford blouses with cardigans and saddle shoes. (She was *so* big into monograms and they were *so* very Connecticut.) I wanted tailored skirts, shift dresses with darts, and sweaters that showed off my developing shape.

For a thirteenth birthday gift, my girlfriend Wendy's mother took us on an after-school shopping spree and bought us both make-up—light face powder, rouge, eyeliner and lipstick.

"Hold still, you'll end up with mascara on the end of your nose," Wendy giggled.

While admiring ourselves in her mirror, Wendy's mom came in to add her comments, "You girls look so pretty. What a nice job you both did with your new make-up."

Arriving home later that afternoon feeling beautiful, proud, and grown-up, I hurried to show Mom. Dad happened to catch a glimpse and before I could even open my mouth commanded, "Go upstairs right now and scrub that stuff off your face. You look like a street walker."

While wearing the dreaded cardigan buttoned in the back without a blouse underneath, the groovy style at the time, Father noticed and went ballistic. Everything had to be conservative, completely neutral. He wouldn't consider anything that would draw attention to my blossoming sexuality. No make-up or lipstick, not even a trendy sweater style.

The only liberty he allowed was choosing how to fix my hair. There too, I stretched the limits using peroxide to lighten it a dozen notches or so. Heaven forbid! Dad instructed Mom to rush me to the local beauty salon for it to be dyed all one ugly brown color before anyone should see me. There I was, like every other teenage girl in America, trying to look like Marilyn Monroe; there he was, trying to make me look like Eleanor Roosevelt.

My wants and desires were not outrageous: no *West Side Story* style gang membership, no LSD (like some of the other kids in town), no cheating on tests at school, nor did I act completely insubordinate to my teachers or other adults. Just like the other local kids, I partook in typical adolescent vices: sneaking a smoke now and then while hiding in the bushes down the road; making stupid phone calls to people we didn't know and laughing while they counted the number of sixty-watt light bulbs in their houses; trespassing on the million-dollar properties of people we didn't even know. All pretty innocent stuff.

On Christmas Eve 1960 (ten days after turning fifteen), we were attending a party with my parents when

I suddenly began to cry for what seemed to be no reason. Frustrated that I was interrupting their fun, both my parents became angry with me—but I just couldn't stop hot salty tears from flowing. In a huff we left the party, with Dad telling me all the way home how inconsiderate I was. Right after being sent to my room, the phone rang—GranMum had passed away an hour earlier. *I do believe in telepathy.*

As a freshman in the last year at junior high, I was on top of the world. The national focus was on physical fitness thanks to the new president, John Fitzgerald Kennedy, and that was my game. I excelled on the track, at field hockey, in gym class, and in after school gymnastics.

For sixteen-year-olds, sex was in the air—at least the stirrings of sexual awareness, with desires yet to be fulfilled.

I'd discovered my physical sexuality quite by accident when I experienced an orgasm while climbing ropes in sixth-grade gym class. That sensation was awesome, omnipotent, good and bad all at the same time. Typical of the '60s, girls were supposed to be sexy but asexual until marriage rang the doorbell. However, it was hard not to notice the effect I had on boys. Knowing my sexuality was a powerful tool gave me confidence both on the athletic field and, strangely, in the classroom.

At the same time, it made Dad more protective. Most fathers were this way when their daughters began to bloom, but mine had a hysterical edge. The only way he knew to influence me was by tightening the screws on my life. Dad sought to maintain order by breaking me like a wild horse.

My mother loved me—of that I am sure—although sometimes it felt as if she were more in love with the *idea* of me than with me as a person who experienced emotion and had viewpoints and attitudes. When I didn't live up to the picture of her dream child, she'd report me to the warden for him to deal with, saving the soft parenting for herself—shopping, cooking, gardening, and teaching domestic skills. She made no attempt to understand my emotions or thoughts; life was simply obedience or disobedience. By this standard I was frequently, almost perpetually, disobedient.

Sophomore year I changed schools and now commuted by train to Greenwich. Being separated from most of my junior high friends was hard at first, so in an effort to make new ones and fit in, I took a part in a school play about the Boston Tea Party. Some inventive kid—not me this time—thought that vodka and orange juice would look a lot like tea from the vantage point of the audience. Having unintentionally consumed enough of it to paint the girls' bathroom a lovely shade of orange and bile I 'fessed up, took my lumps, and got suspended from school for two days. Not the way to fit in! At home, I was also beaten, cursed at, humiliated, and ground deep into the terra firma—like a stomped-out cigarette butt—while other kids on that caper got two days playing on the beach.

When the folks took a European vacation that year they left Mother's old auntie to care for Ginny and me. After everyone else was asleep, I carefully opened the bedroom window overlooking the family room roof, climbed out, and slid down the gutter pipe. Then ever so slowly opening the garage door, I put the car in neutral and rolled back into the street before turning the key and driving off. I'd watched my father drive. It didn't appear to be rocket science. And not having a license yet didn't matter either—the typical impulsive, invincible teenager who didn't think things through. But knowing and doing were two different matters. I actually did pretty well getting to the local parking area overlooking the ocean to hang out with my friends. But when it was time to head home I let the clutch out too quickly causing the car to jump backward in short little frog-like leaps. Coming too close to a tree I partially removed and mangled the decorative chrome molding. I was in deep shit! Of course we couldn't own a Chevy or Ford. Oh no! We had to have something stupid nobody'd ever heard of—a Borgward, a German car from a dealership down the street from the Mercedes and Ferrari lots that Dad drooled over whenever he drove by.

Thank God for "surrogate" Uncle Walter. Walter and Gusta weren't actually related to my parents but were friends who acted as aunt and uncle to us. Their home, in a neighboring town, was small with two bedrooms. Ginny and I looked forward to spending time with them every few weeks. Gusta had worked as a music teacher and, although retired, patiently taught us the magic in the ivory keys. Walter worked at a local hardware store and owned all sorts of cool tools and stuff. We nailed, glued, and repaired lots of things together over the years. Gusta and Walter were kind, fun to be with, and we loved them.

That night wonderful Uncle Walter bailed me out of the car mess and promised not to tell my parents. Unfortunately my mother's auntie wasn't as understanding. She couldn't wait to spill the beans when my parents returned. I'll let you imagine the punishment for that one!

Planning well in advance what to say with aplomb, I successfully negotiated with my father to go to the senior prom with a boy I'd been sweet on. Dad wasn't too keen on me, a sophomore, going with a senior but Mom actually stood up for me and even took me shopping for a dress. We found a nice white one on which she sewed a pretty yellow sash to brighten it up.

Handsome, redheaded Will arrived in a tuxedo with a yellow rose corsage—we made a lovely couple. Dad cautioned Will to behave himself as we were leaving, "If you know what I mean, and be sure to have her home by eleven"

Will "Yes Sir'd," but once in the car gave me a hard time about having a curfew on his senior prom night. "If

I'd known you had a curfew I would have asked someone else."

Not wanting to disappoint or be rejected I said, "Don't pay any attention to him. It's no big deal. I'll get home when I get home."

Well, we stayed out all night with a group of friends walking the local beach and dancing to music on WINS-1010 blasting from our car radios.

Now I don't remember what time it was when I tried to sneak into the house, but the door was locked. Dad must have been waiting on the other side of the door, for when I quietly squeezed through it, he grabbed me by the arm and a big verbal fight ensued followed by a warning, "One more infraction and I will not allow you back in the house. You will live by our rules or get out! Now go upstairs and clean up. You're expected at breakfast."

Soon after that I made an impulsive and dramatic cry for attention. In reaction to being made to eat my meal off the kitchen floor for the umpteenth time by yelling, "I hate you," I rushed to the cupboard under the kitchen sink and grabbed the first bottle my hand touched. "I'll show you! I'll kill myself, then *you'll* be the one in trouble!" Dramatically tipping the bottle upward I took a big swig of what turned out to be ammonia.

As I swallowed, the liquid burned with a heat so intense it would have been impossible to drink enough of it to fulfill the threat. Bits of tongue quickly clogged my mouth and kept peeling away as I spat them onto the floor. I was painfully sick and now scared to death. Dad rushed me to the emergency room in total silence. The only sound in the car was ca-ca-ca-thew noise I made as I hawked into a dishtowel he'd handed me. It seemed surreal the way the hospital doors opened, folding into themselves automatically, as if they knew I was coming. After shoving a garden hose down my throat, the tall, blonde nurse with the pasted on angelic smile poured pasty-grey liquid down the tube while two other nurses

34

who each had two black stripes on their caps held me down. An intense white light in the center of the ceiling dimmed until all was black. I woke up the next morning to the deep, soothing voice of the psychiatrist. He talked with me for a long time and then scheduled visits for twice weekly before signing my discharge papers.

Talking out my troubles felt about the same as vomiting up the ammonia—painful, but better than the alternative of holding it all in, or worse having actually fulfilled the threat I'd made to kill myself. After several weeks, the shrink requested a visit with my father. As soon as the conversation moved from me to him, Dad refused to talk, adamantly insisting I continue therapy alone, and stormed out leaving me there to find my own way home. (No mandated reporting back then.) Dad should have been pleased with the man's ethical desire not to take more of his money but he didn't see it that way. "She isn't fixed yet. I'm paying you. You will see her until she can live by our rules."

And so in the early months of my sophomore year I did homework every other week in the psychiatrist's waiting room. He'd come out, ask if there was anything I wanted to talk about, smile at my wise-ass remark, "Not unless you can help me with chemistry," chat for a short time, then stroll back into his office to do whatever. Both of us knew a relationship with my father couldn't move forward without his participation and Dad was absolutely not talking. He was always right. It was others who were wrong, others who needed fixing, not him.

That psychiatrist did more good for me than many would give him credit for. By affirming that I wasn't totally "messed up" and encouraging me to experience my emotions and trust my intuition, he fostered the confidence I needed to believe in myself.

While rebelling against my adoptive parents' abuse, thoughts of my birth parents again entered my mind.

Imagining a tall, dark haired, blue-eyed, strong and loving birthfather, as well as a beautiful, smiling, blonde-haired birthmother who would hug and kiss me and unrealistically let me do mostly what I wanted, I wrote a long letter to the adoption agency requesting that they return me to my real parents—the best-case scenario.

Father intercepted the letter. Angry, hurtfully he said, "It won't do any good to mail that. Your parents are dead, and they wouldn't want you anyway—you're such a horrid child."

Adoption was irreversible!

## When She Was Bad She Was Horrid

Summer 1962 – Old Greenwich, Connecticut – First Congregational Church

I'd never been a clock-watcher but on this night there wasn't a choice. I was with a bunch of kids in a church social hall on a balmy night in July, but instead of being able to concentrate on my lines and partake in the revelry, I focused on the big wall clock whose hands seemed to move in fast-forward.

Play practice was still going on even though it was already 8:30, quittin' time, but we still had work to do.

That didn't matter to my dad. He was being magnanimous simply by allowing me to go out at all. *Eight fifty-five. Shit!* Practice was over and yet for me, things were only beginning. No way could I run home in five minutes. No way at all. He'd said nine o'clock—ever so close didn't matter. Black and white: right and wrong. One minute past nine was wrong; it might as well have been 9:01 the next morning.

I considered calling but that would lead nowhere. For him to allow me to stay out a few minutes longer would involve a reconsideration of his original position, a gray area, a nuanced thought that might appear weak and indecisive. He was not indecisive—to him such a thing was weak-minded and no one must ever think that of him.

Catching a ride with a friend might have saved precious minutes but still would not have stacked the cards in my favor.

37

*The minister.* Who couldn't trust a minister? Who would ever cast doubt upon the veracity of a tale backed up by a man of the cloth?

"Reverend, could you please give me a ride home?" I asked. "My father worries if I'm out alone." It was a white lie but a plausible one. I was a pretty sixteen-year-old girl with a blossoming figure. The pastor might have felt that my father was being overly and unreasonably protective, but men were allowed to feel that way about their females. In the early '60s, the feminist movement hadn't been born, no Gloria Steinem, no Betty Friedan. I was female and thus a possession of my father much as my mother was. Besides, how do you tell the minister that your father might kill you if you're late?

The nine o'clock curfew was my father's concession to allowing me out at all having already been fully grounded for some minor transgression. But that was why seeing minutes tick by on the dashboard clock I chewed my fingernails as the minister took his sweet time driving the usual six minute route home. Finally we pulled into the driveway.

Quickly opening the door, I said, "Thank you Reverend. I'll see you tomorrow at practice."

"Good night, Carol," he said, and giving a small wave out the window, he backed out of our driveway having no idea he was dropping me off in hell.

I was now ten minutes late.

Just as there was no handbook to guide fathers on how to raise their adoptive daughters, there was no handbook on what to do when you were sixteen and tossed out of your house.

Perhaps that wasn't so unusual in some locales but in affluent Riverside, fathers weren't prone to physically tossing their daughters to the curb, calling them whores and locking the doors on them. The bastard put me through a lot but I'd given it right back.

Hot salty tears stung my eyes as my feet propelled me forward by rote. I screamed out loud into the blackness of night, cursing my father over and over.

Leaning against the tree at the end of our street I thought: *my birth parents never would have treated me like this. Why did they have to die? Why did these hateful controlling people adopt me?* They act like self-appointed saints having done me a favor and expecting, no, demanding gratitude. *Why? Oh, why?*

Eventually I walked with a clearer head, flipping an internal switch that turned on my defense mechanisms, and stuffed the hurt deep inside. A plan. I needed a plan.

GranMum and GranPop were dead and I now desperately missed them more than ever. They'd have intervened on my behalf with Dad, perhaps softening his stance toward me, or letting me live with them in Lake George away from here and his wrath. Mom's parents might take me in, but not at this time of night and not if they thought Dad would find out.

A plan began to formulate.

My current boyfriend Chris was the one person I most wanted to see at that moment. Reaching the train station I dialed his number from the pay phone on the platform and managed to sob out enough of the story: "Fight—parents—train station—come get me." I couldn't go home.

His gentle voice calmed me as he said, "Give me twenty minutes. I've got to explain this to my parents and tell them where I'm going."

The station bench was hard as granite, the night a dark abyss; I was on the verge of slipping over the emotional edge again and barely hung on while reviewing what had just gone down.

The jerk had called me a liar. Understandable. But how did I get from a teenager with too much make-up to a whore? What was that all about? He couldn't possibly know about the flirtation with the gymnastics coach...

Always athletic I could usually be found hanging upside down or climbing somewhere. The perfect channel for my abundant energy while in junior high turned out to be gymnastics. Like many of the other girls I thought the coach an Adonis with his wavy brown hair, hazel eyes, and buff body. We all swooned over and fantasized about him.

My father granted permission for me to stay after school for training. Tumbling and dance came naturally and I excelled, with Coach frequently praising my progress and encouraging me to push myself, even suggesting I set my sights on the Olympics. His flattering attention was total inflation. Privilege, feeling special, and a higher sense self-worth flooded my whole being.

I trusted Coach and somewhere along the way told him about my father's abuse. After listening sympathetically he gave me a Kleenex and one of those it'll-be-OK hugs then walked me to the gymnasium door. Over the next several practices, his hugs came more often and lasted longer making me feel appreciated and cared for, understood.

Late one afternoon when I was the last student to put away my equipment, Coach called me into his office. Facing me he placed both of his hands on my shoulders, smiled sincerely and said, "Carol, you're doing exceptionally well, especially on the vaulting apparatus. I'd like you to do a solo demonstration in the show next month and I've signed you up to go with us to the Olympic try-outs in New Jersey."

Elated and pleased by his compliment I let him pull me closer for a hug—only this time it was a full body hug accompanied by a stirring deep within me. As I tipped my head back to look at him, he kissed me. Not on the cheek, but on the lips.

Pulling back, at first I resisted, knowing it wasn't right. His lips were sweet and soft. I'd kissed a few boys before but this kiss had a passion and hunger to it I'd not experienced before and without another thought I succumbed, kissing him back and felt a stirring in him too.

The scene plagued me all that night and for a few days afterward. Shame and excitement conflicting, I chose avoidance by skipping a scheduled practice. But when the opportunity arose to be alone with him again, excitement won out. Our office trysts continued over the rest of the school year progressing from kissing to kissing-and-petting. Conscience called to me but not loudly enough, so fooling myself into thinking he was a knight in shining armor come to rescue the fair damsel from her abusive father and his controlling rules, I did nothing to stop it.

Could Coach have mistaken pleas for help as flirtatious invitations? Did he wish to compensate for what I'd endured at home, or did he intentionally play on my weaknesses from an abusive home situation? Fantasizing that he loved me, I was devastated when the school year—and the relationship—ended.

Were hurt and depression so obvious? Could Dad have read my mind or body language? No one, not even my best friend, knew about the relationship with Coach. Did Dad know? Was that why he'd labeled me a whore? Or did it go deeper than that? Was my birth mother a whore for having a baby out of wedlock, so I must be one too? Guilty by association?

Car tires crunched into the parking lot. I ran into Chris's arms sobbing anew as he stroked my hair and patiently listened to all the gory details.

He might have been overwhelmed and unsure of himself, but his body felt strong and his demeanor decisive. "Mom told me to bring you home. We'll sort things out in the morning."

Anger and vulnerability began to subside as we drove to Greenwich.

His parents were wonderful. The warm engulfing hug his mother gave relaxed my tense shoulders while the hot drink she placed in my hand calmed a nervous stomach. His mother soon settled me under a feather-light comforter in their guest room but I tossed and turned most of the night, visited by the stone mattress nightmare. Too soon the light of morning danced through the open window. I lay in bed heavy-hearted as the salty smell of bacon wafted in the air.

Chris's mother called, "Carol, time to wake up. There's a robe in the closet. Come have something to eat."

Sitting to the right of me at their oak kitchen table Chris took my hand, squeezed it, then loaded his plate. Over breakfast his mother gently dragged the details out of me with her soft voice and an occasional pat on the hand or arm.

One night in their comfortable home morphed into two, then three. Chris's parents were understanding and hospitable, but Chris was a preppie and came from a prominent Greenwich family, while I was a nouveau riche kid who'd been thrown out of her house. His parents had to think that this whole thing just didn't look right and in the upper class and upper-middle class Eastern suburbs everything always needed to look right.

They never said anything though, for they were well bred and ours was a perpetually oppressed uptight society. Paint on a smile, drink a Manhattan, play some golf, and keep up appearances. I didn't fit in there, in Robotland, the place that would later be fictionalized as the home of the *Stepford Wives*. To me life wasn't all about keeping up appearances and that, among other things, was one source of my rebellion.

Actually it was my mother Margaret—the status-seeker—who truly fit in. She never engaged in controversy, never confronted, chose never to rock the boat and instead feigned indifference until it became a way of life. She always kept up with the "Joneses," was always conscious of how she dressed (even dressing Glenn by shopping and picking out his clothes for him), joined the garden, bridge, and yacht clubs and cared about being "proper." Fitting in.

The paradox was that most of our wealthy neighbors didn't give a damn whether she fit in, or about hands-on parenting. Their kids drank and smoked and got into all kinds of trouble. Yet they seemed rather unperturbed by it. To the other denizens of Riverside and Greenwich, such adolescent traumas were simply irritants, nothing to get all red in the face about, nothing to scream or beat people over. They had an inbred sense of personal satisfaction and confidence based upon their loftier upbringing. In that way my father was like a volatile, paranoid Jay Gatsby ever fearful he would be found out as not being of "their kind."

Certainly other parents threatened to, or actually did, throw their kid out. But wasn't it like that classic little-child cry for attention wherein the tot folds up his belongings in a scarf tied to a stick and then walks down the road, plodding along hobo-slow so that Mom will come running after him telling him to come back? With other parents the scene lasted for all of thirty minutes tops. It was a threat—a dare—not a reality.

But I'd been gone from home for almost a week already. No one looked for me; no one called; no one even tried. I was the horrid little girl of Wadsworth's nursery rhyme my parents so often repeated when referring to me:

"There was a little girl, Who had a little curl,
Right in the middle of her forehead.

43

CAROL LILLIEQVIST WELSH

When she was good, She was very good indeed,
But when she was bad, she was horrid."

    This was real. This crazy, freaking daydream was
real—sixteen, soon to be a senior in high school, living
in an upscale suburban American paradise and now
unceremoniously out on my own ass. I wanted to wake
up. I kept waiting for Allen Funt to step out from
behind a tree and say, "You're on *Candid Camera,*" or for
someone to scoop me up and whisk me away to another
world. But no, because of ten minutes I'd never get
back, no matter what I said or did—*ten lousy minutes*—my
life changed forever.

1962 – 1964

Training Wheels

July 1962 – Greenwich, Connecticut

My new life was thrust on me suddenly, giving such little time to make big decisions, yet an endless string of time and decisions was what appeared before me. Loneliness descended like a cold fog as I realized I'd become completely untethered. Even when people were near I felt completely alone yet under scrutiny, as if living on the wrong side of a one-way mirror.

Thoughts became twisted—blame, rationalization, fabrication—and sometimes I wondered if my father had ever wanted me to begin with, or had he acquiesced to pressures from Margaret and society? Did he expect me to rise to the occasion and move forward with my life? Or did he hope I'd be turning tricks in Times Square, fulfilling his labeling?

The first thing was to find a place to live.

"Boarding house" is a strange term. In 1962, boarding houses were common. Even affluent towns such as Riverside and Greenwich had them. They were not necessarily flophouses for derelicts but mostly served elderly widows and widowers, as well as a few "lifelong bachelors" and "elderly spinsters."

The Stanton House was a gangly white Victorian mansion catering to travelers who visited Greenwich for short stays, but also housed a rather sizeable stable of residential regulars. I'd noticed the sign for it two years earlier during my one brush with the mental healthcare system as I waited impatiently for the Post Road light to change en route to my therapist's office.

47

The short, stout woman who ran the Stanton House eyed me warily even though I cut a respectable-enough figure. When she questioned me, while not giving up all my personal information, I eagerly provided my employment data, proud that I had a job and money of my own. I paid the first two weeks rent in advance— twelve dollars total—and when pressed, stated that I attended school, though which school and why was none of her business. A number of business, secretarial, and community colleges, as well as beauty schools abounded in the area.

At a time when Dad would be at work, I mustered enough courage to call my mother and ask for my belongings. Reluctantly she agreed to put them out on the front stoop as long as they were gone by the time he got home. Even though Dad wasn't home she wouldn't allow me in "his house."

This was real; this was permanent. I really was banished.

The discussion with my mother went nowhere. "There's nothing else to talk about. You'll get your things and that's it. Be sure to get them tomorrow or I will throw them away." Click. Maybe she was afraid Dad would find out we'd spoken which would have severe repercussions for her.

I never really understood my mother and can only speculate that Dad seemed to have cowed her as completely as he'd attempted to cow me, but with her, the domination was complete. Mom saw what was happening and went along with it for the sake of self-preservation. It would have been just too scary to stand up to Dad for fear of being beaten or disowned—or divorced, the worst possible outcome, given the times. She got from him what she most wanted: marriage, money, and social standing. What she gave up in exchange was me.

I found all my clothes in a few cardboard boxes stacked by the driveway. She'd included a couple of keepsakes and a small handful of photographs—proof of my childhood existence—and the black-and-white panda bear that meant more to me than she knew. I fantasized it had been given to me by the world's most divine mother who'd christened it with tears of love symbolizing an idealized parental love that would never truly be mine. That mother was not Margaret, the woman who raised me. It was some other woman, my deceased birthmother, and I clung to her through the bear, holding it and rubbing it so many times that it became bald, beautiful, and loved only by me just as I'd imagined I had been by her.

A Rescue — of Sorts

Dropping out of school never really occurred to me. This was my last year and in spite of the situation, I was doing a pretty good job of figuring things out.

Even so, I needed people to stand on my side in this war my father and I waged against each other, to prove outwardly that I was right and he was wrong—his labeling of me vindictive; that it wasn't right for an adoptive parent to permanently abandon his chosen child. And I needed to know that my own two feet could support me, that strength and bravery were within reach.

The isolation of being on my own became especially hard after Chris went back to prep school. Nights equaled loneliness. The only people in the Stanton house were the other residents with whom I had nothing in common. Sticking my nose in a good book or listening to Alan Freed play Rock-n-Roll on WINS-1010 New York provided my only escape.

My father had been transporting me to my weekend job at a florist shop. Now this was proving to be a hassle because the train was expensive and it was too far to walk. A solution presented itself when a waitressing job opened up at a sandwich-and-ice-cream shop called Nielson's. The hours worked with school and the location on the corner of the Post Road and Field Point Road was convenient, just a few minutes walk from school.

Deliberately I began to change my circle of friends, seeking out older people from work who considered me a peer despite my age. This soothed the pain a bit but gave the kids in high school even more reason to talk about me.

No other teen at my high school was completely without parents or living on his or her own—only me. Rumors spread; I was accused of throwing wild parties and having orgies. Dream on! In actuality, my bedroom was tiny and I shared a bathroom with an untold number of others. The Waldorf Astoria, it wasn't. A lot of girls giggled, suggesting I had it made while they were making out in the backseat of some boy's family Plymouth. As flattering as they made my life out to be, I was still dating Chris when he was home and my rule was to never bring anyone to my small place. So I would also have been in those same backseats wrestling around in the darkness, hoping not to get caught by some policeman cruising Lover's Lane.

Having been a precocious child I somehow knew from an early age being cute could get me places and capitalized on it. My mother said that when I was young I could wrap father around my little finger and get him to do anything for me. Obviously, that changed.

Precocious yes, but promiscuous? No. Well maybe just a little. I wasn't into one-night stands and usually dated a boy exclusively for weeks or months. "Going all the way" was not to be trifled with and most experiences were still primarily about making out.

I was by far the youngest person living in the Stanton House. The whole boarding-house scene could weird me out if I let it. After work I'd climb the fire escape and enter my room at the rear of the fourth floor through a window to avoid having to tiptoe past the checker-playing elderly gentlemen sitting in the first-floor living room, watching the door for anyone who entered. Not that anything was wrong with these senior citizens, but I viewed them as leering older gents with only me, and their well-thumbed copies of *Playboy* and the *Sports Illustrated* swimsuit issue, to fill their fantasies. My life was like a *Snow White* story where instead of an evil stepmother I had a father who hated me and now I lived with the Seven Liver-Spotted Old Men. The awkward part was that Snow White never had to go to school each day and answer questions about what it was like to live with Grumpy, Dopey, and Doc.

Sometimes though, it was fun to hang out with the old guys. They'd explain football plays to me while we watched on the TV in the big living room we all shared—or *they* shared, as I otherwise pretty much stayed away for fear of having to enter into conversations that would inevitably be prying in nature.

Living alone provided a lot of benefits though. No longer did the pressures of living with my father linger over my head. No more clock-watching except for wanting time to move faster toward the end of the day at my waitress job. On the other hand, I'd gone through my entire life being told what to do and how to do it by the consummate micromanager. Getting used to making my own decisions was an adjustment.

Cooking on a little illegal hot plate was fun. I could eat all the not-so-healthy chips and pickles I wanted when it struck my fancy. Most of the time my diet was well balanced with the occasional indulgence of chocolate or soda, both of which were forbidden at home. But I needed to learn on my own how the real world worked—laundromats, bank accounts, writing checks, and balancing a budget. Other kids were taught some of these skills as they went off to college. Not I.

School felt different too. I became more responsible in many areas and more irresponsible in others. My grades dropped. I took up smoking. Oh, other kids smoked but none of the "good" kids did.

Instead of thinking about school and phone calls to my girlfriends, I worried about what to have for dinner, being certain to have clean clothes, and whether my paycheck would cover the rent.

I had planned to go to college. In grade school I'd been an avid fan and reader of Helen Wells' *Cherry Ames* nurse series and aspired to become a nurse. Loving gym class and being a good athlete led me to consider teaching physical education and I had been active in the future teachers and nurses clubs. But now I was off to work as soon as the final bell rang. During study halls, however, I hung out with the short, stocky school nurse who found things for me to do. Trusting her, I shared what I thought was safe.

October 1962

The school authorities had discovered I was living on my own. Did the school nurse have a hand in it? Or did Carolyn and Bill Richardson call them (my confidantes for whom I still babysat)?

Apparently no matter how well or maturely I was handling life; an un-emancipated minor couldn't be enrolled in school unless living under the roof of an adult. Sleepy, Sneezy, and the other old men didn't count.

A truant officer arranged for a few counseling visits with Child Welfare in the red building next to McArdle's Greenhouses, close enough to school that I could walk there. The caseworker contacted my parents and arranged an interview and inspection of their home—as if they were adopting a child rather than tossing one out.

The Child Welfare worker also visited some of the neighbors including Carolyn and Bill Richardson. During the interview with Carolyn and Bill, the caseworker stated, "If someone could take her in— grandparents, godparents, anyone—we wouldn't have to recommend placing her in foster care." *What had my father done? Greeted them at the door with a bloody meat cleaver?*

Carolyn blurted, "Well, she can live with us from now on."

(I wish I'd known about these conversations at the time, for I would have been grateful that someone in authority finally saw the true color of my father's stripes.)

53

The outcome of this home study, coupled with reports from the counseling sessions, was that I moved into Carolyn and Bill's guest room, becoming a foster child of sorts.

The guest room was comfortable, decorated in browns and greens, unlike my periwinkle blue room down the street. Lying awake at night with scenarios playing in my head, I thought about seeing my parents and having another confrontation with Dad. Practicing what to say to him tormented me the first several weeks with the Richardsons was sleeplessly stressful.

In spite of being only a few houses away we somehow managed to avoid each other. As much as I wished to avoid a confrontation, subconsciously I desperately wanted all this to be over, for Dad to walk down the street, ring the doorbell, command me to gather my things and come home. To wrap me in his arms and say he loved me. That never happened either.

The Richardsons laid out a few common sense rules but nothing as strict as what I'd been used to. Family space was to be respected, kept picked up and tidy. My room was mine. I could arrange and leave it any way I liked as long as it was safe. In exchange for living with them, I would take care of Harry when I got home from school and on evenings when they needed to work late. Both Carolyn and Bill were attorneys with busy practices. Sounds of laughter and humor permeated the house—something foreign to my ears. And we talked about anything openly and comfortably. They expected me to participate with cooking and helping in the kitchen as they made a point of eating dinner together casually (no more squaring my meal as I ate). Sitting at the kitchen counter or dining table as often as possible, we were relaxed and truly interested in what each other had to say. But the best part of living with them was Harry. The adorable, wavy dark-haired four-year-old idolized me and followed me around like a puppy— different from the situation with Ginny.

It was strange to live down the street from her, see her walking to school and know she was forbidden to have anything to do with me. How different we'd become. In the time leading up to my eventual severance from the family, she had chosen sides. I granted her absolution to a certain degree due to self-preservation— as she figured out how to survive in that household. Thus, when I got the boot, she made no significant effort to stay in touch with me, and every effort to avoid me, per Glenn's instructions.

This hurt just as much as my parents' rejection. It wasn't fair to hold a grudge toward her for not risking her own position in the family to support me, but still I wanted her to maintain ties, even if secretly.

In spite of Bill and Carolyn's support, senior year in high school felt like living in the *Twilight Zone*. I was there, but not—my thoughts were mostly of the future and what it would hold.

Sometimes my mind wandered. Was my father waiting for some grand gesture from me—an apology for being ten minutes late or simply for being me? But no, he wasn't waiting for anything from me. I was ancient history to him. He'd moved on.

When someone closes the door on you so emphatically, after a time your own resolve stiffens and you don't want to be the one who ends up on your hands and knees begging for reconciliation. Dad and Mom could have found me easily, started the healing process. After all, we were practically living next to each other. But my parents were intractable.

How could he simply have dismissed his own child in such a way? He'd chosen me; we'd known each other for sixteen years. I was not a concept without history or personality to him, I had been his daughter all that time and he, my father. There'd been a lot of good times along with the bad. Yet none of that mattered to him.

One set of grandparents was dead but Grandma and Grandpa Russell lived in town. I'd kept in touch with them without letting my parents find out. But I never asked them to intercede on my behalf—a combination of my own stubbornness, and knowing that should they confront Glenn directly, the result would be rejection of them too. So when it was safe, I'd sneak over to their house for warm cookies and love, though I was careful not to go too often for fear of getting caught.

Early that spring I'd traded in my orthopedic waitress shoes for dress shoes and landed a semi-sit-down job as a telephone operator with Rodgers & Company, a department store in downtown Greenwich. The pay was better, or at least more dependable than tips, and the job more socially respectable than waitressing. The office on the third floor held a classic-style peg switchboard—four-dozen holes with corresponding lights, a headset, and octopus-like cords with plugs on the ends. The switchboard was located next to a table with an overhead pneumatic air system that sent carrying tubes containing sales slips and payments from the merchandise floor up to the office, just like today's drive-through banks. I'd wait for the swoosh-thunk of the carrier amidst the panel buzzing and lights blinking, then turn around, grab the tube, complete the sale (as no cash was kept on the sales floor), stamp and return the receipt—all while hoping to insert the right plug into the right hole on the switchboard. Multitasking at its finest!

June 1963

Graduation went off without a hitch. After throwing my cap in the air, I spotted Glenn and Margaret milling around with a couple of the other parents. They had the *balls* to show up.

Glenn was easy to spot wearing his plaid pants and bright green sports coat; an outfit he thought was dashing but really made him look like a clown and detracted from his handsomeness. Margaret stood expressionless next to him in her navy polka dotted dress that looked like someone threw paper circles from a three-hole punch at her, randomly matching the pattern of moles on her face and arms.

I longed to see them but kept a reasonable distance knowing I might break down if I got too close, or reach out and risk a touch. Approaching, just close enough to catch a whiff of Dad's carrot-cake-batter Old Spice aftershave, I said, "Hi! It was nice of you to come."

"We're here at the Hamilton's invitation to see Lee graduate." Dad's words severed anew.

"Oh! Well, I hope you enjoyed yourself," I replied sarcastically, spinning on my heel and walking away as erectly as possible but feeling like a beaten dog with its tail between its legs.

September 1963

Having had a full-time job for several months I'd managed to squirrel away some money and was making an adequate transition into adulthood. Now I wanted more.

With Carolyn and Bill's blessing, I rented a studio apartment on the third floor of a house in Greenwich where the owners lived on the first floor. It was liberating. I saw myself as a free spirit with training wheels still fastened to my life bicycle. At least now it was by my own choice.

I was finally the swingin' single girl of all the rumors from the year before. High school girlfriends drifted from my life, many of them going off to college. Making new friends who were mostly older, I soon began to mimic them. But I still stuck to dating one boy at a time rather than picking up guys and forgetting them the next day. I'd learned by then how to get a nice evening out of the experience not just a trek to Lookout Point. I was becoming more mature, more experienced and so were the boys—some of them could even be referred to as men.

While still living under the Richardson's roof, I'd met a wonderful man. Frank came from a solid, loving family. Our relationship blossomed over several months. He was fun to be with, wasn't freaked out or turned off by my family situation, and bolstered my self-esteem by building me up rather than putting me down. We became serious. Life was getting better.

One evening while we were sitting on his sofa Frank stood up unexpectedly and pulled something out of his pocket then sat back down with a Cheshire Cat grin on his round, handsome face. Pulling me closer he kissed me passionately as he slid off the sofa and knelt before me. Deep brown teddy-bear eyes gazing into mine, he took my hand and clumsily slipped an engagement ring on my finger asking, "Will you marry me, Carol?"

I jumped off the sofa almost knocking him over. "Yes, yes," I said, lunging at him, landing us both flat on the floor.

*Engaged: something to be proud of!* Marriage meant salvation. This was what young ladies who didn't go to college were supposed to do—get married. Too bad I couldn't share my news with Glenn and Margaret or, more accurately, throw it in their faces.

Carolyn and Bill were happy for us, although I'm sure they had their reservations. They could see my excitement over being engaged was a reaction to the circumstances, yet were wise enough to support me, wish me well, and keep their concerns to themselves. Carolyn must have prayed I'd come to my senses and not make any mistakes that would lead to unhappiness later in life, but we never talked about it. They knew even if I didn't that I still had some growing up to do.

We proceeded with plans for our wedding, acting like young lovers do when preparing for a life event, partying with our friends, shopping for household items, talking about the future, and making out a lot—even going all the way. I was finally headed in the right direction, or so I thought for a while.

Perhaps it was Carolyn's prayers or another kind of divine intervention, but as the date for the wedding drew closer my feet got colder and colder. Frank was wonderful. He was everything one could ask for in a husband yet dreams invaded my sleep—stone blankets pressed down even harder. My inner voice warned, *don't go through with this.* Even teenagers can dig deep and pay attention to their intuition. Frank loved me but I wasn't *in love* with him; I was infatuated with him and what marriage could bring. Love required more maturity than I was capable of at that time. No, this was not love. It was a good time, it was wanting to be rescued and prove my respectability—wanting to prove my father wrong.

"Life is what happens while you're making other plans"—isn't that how the line goes? Days dripped by like a leaky faucet while I shrank my world, making disappointments fewer. Long-term planning involved what to wear to work the next day or what to pack for lunch. Anything much further into the future than that was too much to think about.

Partying blocked out life. I smoked more, drank more—threw caution to the wind. At one party a guy I'd never met showed an interest in me. He was a great dancer, attractive and, like me, on the rebound from a relationship he thought was serious which gave us something in common.

This fling lasted several weeks before he shipped off to Vietnam just like tens of thousands of young men around the country. It was my pleasure to give him a proper send-off. Who said I didn't do my patriotic duty for my country?

## CAROL LILLIEQVIST WELSH

May 1964

The boy had been gone five weeks. He hadn't sent any letters or called. And my period was late.

Lemonade

When you're a teenager, alone and pregnant, you go through the first four stages of grief—denial, anger, bargaining, and depression. Also include confusion, embarrassment, shame, and hysteria or any other emotion you want to throw into the stew before reaching acceptance.

I'd been so careful. Certainly aware of when I'd be most vulnerable. I didn't think the risk was high when we'd had sex. But giving in to his protests I hadn't always insisted he use a condom either. Birth control pills were available but you needed parental permission as they were fairly new and primarily prescribed for married couples wanting to plan their pregnancies. Just my luck it happened with a boy who wasn't even in the United States. Nor would he be coming home any time soon.

What was I going to do now? *Shit!*

I tried calling him. After all kinds of military phone transfers someone finally put me through to a major who informed me that he had not yet left the States but was in California getting packed up and ready for action. The major said he'd do his best to have him call me before he shipped out.

"Do you want to leave a message?"

The question was almost comical. What are the two things you don't want to tell someone over the telephone via a third party? That there's been a death in the family, or someone's going to be a father.

What could I say to this total stranger who, at the time, also sounded uncannily like my father?

61

So I left my name and number then waited, and waited, and waited some more, measuring insanity by the tasks I'd accomplished as each hour and day passed. I became manic. Calling again and again, I frantically stuffed change into the phone's coin slot, each time asking to speak to anyone who might get a message through to him. Attempting to verify whether he was still in California or had already left the country, I desperately pestered and irritated people all up and down the military chain of command.

For a time I'd get my wits about me, then lose it and be on the damn phone again, not knowing what else to do. Finally I'd just sit and stare at the silent phone, numb as a beaten thumb. At some point I was so distraught it even seemed as if my relationship was with the phone booth.

Hanging up for the umpteenth time I turned to letter writing instead. Yeah, that was the way to go—a letter. In Jane Austen books the lovers always sent each other long, flowery letters. "Dear Mr. Darcy, it is with wingéd heart that I delight in informing you your seed has not gone unfertilized deep within my womanliness, and that we shall be as one forever in undying love upon your return from the battlefront. Godspeed my love, and let my fervor for you guide you through the dark night of war." Oh, and by the way what was your first name again?

The letter never got sent; the phone never rang.

Instead, I packed. Something inside of me (no pun intended) intuitively said, "Get out of Greenwich." I was pregnant and couldn't get my virginity or innocence back—*you can't shove a genie back into a bottle*—but I wasn't a whore, and that was what the town would think if they found out.

Moreover I couldn't bring shame onto Carolyn and Bill after all they had done for me, and if my parents ever found out, Dad would see it as proof that he was right.

Despondent, tears flowed down my cheeks as I thought, God I really screwed up this time. I sure as hell didn't want to be a parent—not without a husband. One was supposed to be a wife before a mother. Someone should be caring for me not the other way around. I didn't want this baby!

But I'd made lemonade out of life's sour lemons so far and I'd devise a way to deal with this, too.

*Slowly walking across a meadow of vibrant wildflowers—blue lupine, yellow buttercups, red Indian paintbrush, and purple clover, I focus on the not-too-distant woods. At the tree line, the vegetation changes to tall pines interspersed with lacy-leafed ferns, duff covering the forest floor. The air grows cooler on my exposed skin as I enter the woods and inhale an earthy odor. Ahead, a fire throws out heat from inside a stone ring. Inner surfaces of the stones are charred, while the outer ones are smooth and gray. A larger stone ring surrounds the smaller one and has an opening facing east.*

*Passing through the opening, my skin warms. I rub my hands together as the coals glow red, flaring every once in a while, yellows and blues leaping from the nearly spent logs that hiss in song.*

*A woman sits opposite where I stand. "The heat is healing," she says, somehow able to know my thoughts. Although she's sitting, I can see she's slightly taller than me. Her almost-white hair is pulled high in a bun, a few wisps escaping at the sides emanating a regal presence. A serene face, with fair, milky skin, holds a naggingly familiar mouth and jaw. It's her gaze that draws me in, gathering strength and intensity, eyes as blue as an ocean on a cloudless day, I sense a depth of wisdom equally as immeasurable.*

*Our eyes lock. Nodding, hearing her in my mind, I sit crossing my legs at the ankles, and draw in a deep breath.*

*The two of us are silent for a long time as we stare at the fire. Occasionally, we gaze into each other's eyes, searching.*

*Breaking the silence telepathically, "What brings you, child?"*

*"I've really messed up. My parents don't want me. I'm pregnant, and don't want the baby."*

*The woman lifts a bony hand slightly, gesturing for me to come closer. Rising, I walk around the fire to stand before her. Lovingly she opens her arms, gathers and holds me to her breast, gently rocking back and forth, back and forth, comforting, soothing.*

*"Have courage and be brave. Everything has a purpose!"*

*Soon I feel myself melting into her, releasing all resistance, as I accept her nurturance, her love, and soon fall into a deep sleep in her lap—believing I am strong and protected.*

Waking with the dream still vivid in my mind, I experienced an overwhelming gratitude. Miraculously, as if words had been spoken out loud, I knew what needed to be done.

The Greenwich Library offered a good selection of books on pregnancy. Discovering a hiding place between the stacks I'd sit with two books on my lap, one on pregnancy and the other on something else, my antennae on high alert for anyone who might recognize me. Should they approach I'd cover one book with the other pretending to be learning about blueberry bushes, or skydiving, anything that would act as a decoy.

I knew so few of the facts about childbirth and all that went along with it. My mother never sat me down for any sex talks, and Dad certainly hadn't. Hell, Mom hadn't even taught me about menstruation! I'd listened to the segregated lecture in sixth grade but mostly giggled through it with the other girls rather than paying attention. My first period came while I was at school, and I'd been frightened and confused. The school nurse had provided supplies and educated me with the facts. Everything else I'd gleaned on the street—the beautiful, tree-lined suburban street. Obviously, I'd managed to learn the basic ins and outs of the act (pun intended) but I really didn't know anything about birthin' babies! For now a girdle ensured secrecy, as it did for so many other unwed pregnant girls of the '50s and '60s. It did a good job of sucking me in—in all the right places—but boy, was it uncomfortable and a pain in the butt when I had to pee.

But how long would it be before I'd show? That was the sixty-four thousand dollar question. I'd been discarded like a worn out old toy, was on my own, and now I was pregnant out of wedlock. This was too much shame.

I needed to get outta Dodge. The little girl in me still hoped for that long-awaited reconciliation with Dad while the grown-up woman wasn't going to be shamed, or worse, found out and again labeled a whore, or forced into one of the hush-hush homes for unwed mothers I had heard horror stories about.

So I looked for a different job and a new place to live far enough away so that no one would know me.

With my wondrous switchboard-waitress-salesclerk skills, job hunting was fairly easy. A company in Darien hired me to operate the switchboard and, answering an ad in a local newspaper for a roommate, I found a new home in North Stamford—all in the same day.

In ignorance, I imagined waking up any given morning to find myself suddenly a walking dirigible so I wanted a plan, a plausible story. Buying a cheap and simple wedding band, as generic as they come, suddenly I was married. And my husband (whose name time has blocked from my memory) had just shipped off to Vietnam to make the world safe for God and democracy. Tragic, but he would be so proud and happy when he returned and found his little bundle of joy— about which he knew nothing. (Truthfully, he probably didn't remember my name either!)

65

Being married was certainly reasonable. Old men weren't being sent overseas to die just young boys with young wives, as young as me. And so a new persona emerged: a war wife, disguising my shame by living a lie.

## Illegal Procedure

Maria quickly accepted me and my condition and soon enjoyed playing the part of an older sister taking responsiliblity for looking out for me as well as telling me what to do. From Italian ancestry, she was shorter than I but had been blessed with dark curly hair and an olive complexion that I was jealous of sometimes. Acting like a female Mafia boss she'd bark commands to motivate both of us. "Come on, we'll do the dishes now." Her wonderful dry sense of humor made up for the bossiness of those orders. After eight hours of plugging holes and looking at flashing lights, laughter was good medicine.

With her, there were no lies or false fronts. I desperately needed someone to talk with about the pregnancy and its myriad details—and Maria was there for me, spending many long nights patiently listening, playing the part of devil's advocate, keeping confidences, and going along with made-up stories.

Eventually I settled on abortion, an ugly procedure, but one that would resolve my unwanted pregnancy. Since I didn't identify with the life growing inside me— it wasn't a baby, just a pregnancy—it seemed the only logical choice.

Abortions were illegal in 1964 before *Roe v. Wade*—but the law never stopped abortions from happening. The wealthy could always find nice, clean, professional environments and staff to perform such procedures. Those like me who had fewer financial resources could still find someone somewhere to help us out.

If you wanted a bag of pot you could always find a drug dealer. And if you wanted an illegal abortion, you could do a bit of discreet street research and you would have a name, phone number, and an address. So the necessary connections and arrangements were made.

Maria offered to lend me money for the procedure and provided transportation to the place.

Her car crept along the street as both of us scanned front doors for the right number. "There, that's the place," I said, pointing to an ordinary two story brown house with off-white trim that looked not a lot different from the other houses lining the street. *Just a number, no signs.*

Pulling over, shutting off the engine Maria asked, "Do you want me to go in with you?"

"No. This is something I have to do by myself." My hand on the door latch felt as if it were made of lead.

Steeling myself, erasing all emotion, I climbed the steep, cracked concrete driveway to the entrance in the rear of the building, while *step on a crack and break your mother's back* ran absurdly through my brain.

Heartbeats pulsed in my ears as I firmly gripped the door handle and pulled it toward me, stepping into a wall of medicinal odor. In the dark lobby on a worn wooden reception desk lay an open sign-in register. My spine tingled with uneasiness while my hand shook. Years ago Margaret had told me that Johnson was my birth name and now I felt my nostrils flare as I scribbled "Carol Johnson" at the bottom of the list. It never occurred to me to read anyone else's name and hopefully the next person wouldn't either.

Extending her hand the receptionist stated, "That will be three hundred dollars. You have to pay first you know."

Fumbling in my purse for the wad of bills held tightly with a rubber band, I looked up and handed her the money. Then through an open door behind the red-haired woman, I saw a twin bed next to a white metal table with a large white enamel bowl on it that had silver instruments sticking out of it and my throat tightened, eyes bulging out like a chicken being strangled.

"Because you've waited so long to do this, the risks are much higher. You should have come to us months ago. The procedure can still be done but it will take longer and you may experience more problems in the first few days."

Stoic, I felt as if I were behind a one-way mirror able to see the nurse-receptionist and doctor's mouths moving but unable to hear their conversation. Even if I could have read lips, this whole thing plagued me and I hung my head low, averting eye contact, rapidly swallowing saliva.

*Would I bleed to death and die there?* If I did, the Richardsons and my estranged parents would find out. My gut wrenched and my pulse quickened as Glenn's words rang in my head: "You're nothing but a damned whore!" Didn't whores get abortions for unwanted pregnancies? Oh, I'd wanted to hurt my father and mother but this was not the way to do it. I simply couldn't let my father win that way.

Turning on my heel, I fled, stumbling down the driveway blinded by tears. Once inside the safety of Maria's car, a modicum of relief washed over me until, wiping my eyes with my palms then blowing my nose, it dawned on both of us that this wasn't going to be over any time soon. I was still pregnant and three hundred dollars poorer.

That night, and for several afterward, I dreamed of being chased by metal instruments. I'd wake sweating with a medicinal smell in my nostrils that affirmed I'd made the right decision in fleeing.

Anyone can run down the realities of the situation. Maria spent hours hashing things over with me. What kind of parent could I be? My role models were horrible. I dreaded being like them. Nature or nurture, it didn't matter. Everything pointed toward my sucking at this job, especially since "mommy" wasn't what I wanted to be. Trapped in this nightmare all I wanted was a life: a good life!

I was doing okay financially by having a roommate. But even if Maria was magnanimous enough not to mind having a tyke around, she certainly wasn't going to help pay for diapers, formula, and childcare. I'd have to go back to work, find another new job right away in order to keep up with expenses.

My mind spiraled while my heart raced. There were no good answers. Shit, there were barely any *reasonable* answers.

The only workable solution left to me was adoption. But I needed a story, and so another falsehood formed. Since everyone at my new job in Darien believed I was married to a guy fighting in Vietnam, I could admit to being pregnant and pretend to eat anything and everything in sight, which would account for my sudden weight gain from shedding the girdle. My co-workers would be happy for me, even become protective since hubby wasn't around.

But what about when I actually had the baby? Returning to work without a baby would mean more fibs.

The simplest solution would be for me to pick up and move before the baby was born, begin *another* new life even further away from familiar eyes and ties.

I was so young and yet was living like some undercover CIA operative surrounded by secrets and intrigue, just wishing it felt as cool as it sounded.

Keeping the baby was never a serious consideration. That thought produced nothing but sweaty palms and reasons why it simply could not be. Single parenting wasn't socially acceptable. Keeping the baby would have been as ridiculous as putting on surgical scrubs and pretending to be a brain surgeon. Maybe if I were to go to medical school and become a doctor, a respectable member of society with a husband

and a big fat income, then perhaps I'd be capable of being a good mother.

In a decade or so, then I might be ready. Maybe if I was still living at home and had support, really was married or had a lucrative career, I would feel differently. But none of this was reality and I had to deal with the situation.

CAROL LILLIEQVIST WELSH

Hope

October 1964

Maria taught me to drive and even let me use her
car to get my license. In my seventh month I quit my
job and used some of my savings to purchase a set of
wheels: a big, black 1949 Plymouth. The old junker
resembled a humpback whale.

The story was that my in-laws, who lived in
California, wanted me to be closer to them so they could
help care for me and the baby—not an unreasonable tale
given my family history—so I'd be moving at the end of
the month. But Hartford was actually my destination.
There I could live out whatever next lie I would tell in
order to cover up my past and present. Then when this
baby was born, I'd move again. My colleagues at work
hosted a baby shower for me and wished me well.

Tears wetted Maria's cheeks as we hugged
awkwardly, then her booming voice commanded, "Take
care of yourself. Good luck, and let me know how it
goes." She then slammed the door with a force that
shook the car. Neither of us suspected we'd never see
each other again.

Heading north I couldn't look in the rearview
mirror, instead I focused on the road and what lay
ahead.

For a studio apartment in a solid, brick warehouse-
type building I paid a month's rent in advance and
cleverly talked the landlord out of a security deposit.
Huge south-facing windows allowed bright sunshine to
flood the dark brick walls making the place less dreary.

72

Picking up a few little items at a flea market, I made the partially furnished studio comfortable and homey.

With nothing but the pregnancy to focus on, all sorts of nagging but common physical maladies plagued me. I was now the dirigible I had feared earlier, walking with the typical pregnant swagger. Having gladly given up my girdle long ago, my belly now stuck straight out with nowhere else on my petite frame for the baby to go. Getting out of bed was hilarious How cool would it be if the mattress came with an eject button?

Fortunately, morning sickness hadn't bothered me because I was too scared to be ill, although during the last few months I ate every meal two or three times because of terrible indigestion. I know where the expression "it repeats on you" comes from. My co-workers had predicted it would be a boy with lots of hair. I didn't care as long as it was over soon.

Carefully I inspected the protrusion and religiously applied cream to the stretched-out skin for there could be no telltale signs left behind.

Emotions became raw. Coming in waves, I would laugh or cry at the drop of a hat, often indulging in self-pity. I wanted my mommy. Well, more accurately my *real* mommy, either my deceased birthmother or some idealized Dream Woman completely unlike Margaret. But the Dream Woman was only in my dreams and came to me randomly. Feeling sorry for myself, hormones raging, I wished for Margaret even though she hadn't been a mother to me for a long time. I also wished to be part of a family once again, for a re-do of the past couple of years.

While in this valley of self pity, another plan began to formulate in my mind.

Holding on to some semblance of sanity, I knew the one thing I couldn't do was show up at my parents' house unmarried and pregnant, or holding a baby. I'd resigned myself to that already. No babies for me. I was doing a good job of avoiding attachment to the life

73

growing inside me and now rushing my own mental timetable, with no one to slow me down, I plotted and planned to spend Christmas back home with my parents—to try for another chance.

It was a little before Thanksgiving with only a month to go. Great timing! For my plan to work, I needed to physically look normal, not as though I'd just delivered a baby. As cinematically as that scene played out in my head—my showing up and Glenn and Margaret throwing their arms around me saying, "We forgive you. We missed you! It's a Christmas miracle!"— it just didn't seem realistic. Groundwork needed to be laid first.

Imagining mother lifting the phone to her ear, I placed a smiling look of love and caring on her moley, buck-toothed face. Taking a deep breath and double-crossing the fingers of my left hand, I dialed. "Hi, this is Carol. Please don't hang up. I'd really like to talk to you."

Surprised, a hint of fear in her voice, she replied, "What is it? You know your father doesn't want us talking to you."

Breathe, Carol. You can do this. "I know, and I'm sorry. I've really missed all of you. It's been hard not being at home."

"That was your choice."

"I know that too, and again, I'm really sorry. Could we start over? Could I just come for few days? A trial run?"

"I doubt your father would allow it. Why don't you go see Carolyn and Bill?"

Ignoring her last suggestion, I said, "Please, please give me another chance. I'll do anything he wants. Couldn't you just ask him?"

After a long silence in which I thought she'd hung up on me, she continued in a more motherly, less secretarial voice, saying, "Well, if he had a good day at work... We'll see."

A glimmer of hope! She'd said, *We'll see*, which usually meant I'd get my way. But that was when I was younger. Still, she hadn't said no.

"Thank you, Mom. Let's hope he says yes. I miss you!"

"Don't thank me yet, Carol. Call me Friday around noon."

Friday couldn't come soon enough. Again double-crossing my fingers, my body damp with sweat, I dialed.

The minute she said hello, I heard a difference in her voice and already knew the answer. "Your father and I have discussed it. He has agreed to a two-day trial but not until after the Christmas holiday."

My throat got that tight, lumpy ache it gets before tears fall as I choked, "Oh, thank you. Thank you, Mom."

"It's all right, Carol. But you'd better behave yourself and do exactly what he tells you! You're on tentative ground here. This is just a trial. It will be up to you to see how far it will go."

"I know. Thank you. I promise to be good!"

After sorting out the few details we hung up. Holy shit! I got the audition! But I'd better not blow it.

One major issue remained to be resolved: this baby was supposed to be born on December twenty-first and by then I knew how pregnancies worked—you can't set your watch by them. Particularly as first pregnancies were known to be late. That wouldn't do!

After arriving in Hartford I'd sought out an OB/GYN and had made clear my intention to adopt. He'd been supportive of my plan but scolded me severely for not having sought prenatal care before then. Eating as healthfully as possible on my budget and exercising regularly, I assured him my physical health was excellent. I'd even cut down considerably on smoking, though I hadn't quite mustered the strength to give it up completely. I just couldn't find the fortitude to tackle an addiction and the pregnancy at the same time.

Now I made an appointment to include him in my plan for reconciliation with the family. I implored that under no circumstances would he contact Glenn and Margaret, explaining the disastrous results should they find out about my pregnancy. Promising to keep my confidence we worked out a payment plan, a referral to an adoption social worker, and talked about an induction date of Friday, December 18th if the baby hadn't come on its own by then. Early enough to assure a normal appearance for the trial visit; late enough in pregnancy that it was safe for the baby to be born. *Whew!*

This guy was a magic genie—a partner in planning.

In hopes of getting this show on the road, I occupied myself over the next weeks by walking, watching soap operas, and awkwardly rock-n-rolling to Alan Freed for hours on end, urging my uterus to contract.

Knowing the end was in sight, I finally allowed myself to consider who this fetus growing inside me might be and couldn't help laughing at a baby with a sense of humor who consistently knocked food and drink off an abdominal table.

Whenever I felt conflicted I'd close my eyes and pray for comfort from the Dream Woman. Unrealistically, I'd elevated my fantasized birthmother to a mythical level, allowing her to be the Dream Woman—panacea to all my ills.

If days were occupied with busyness, nights dragged on. Staring out the big paned windows, pewter clouds like dirty snow banks matching my nocturnal mood, I'd hug my teddy bear and wish for things to be different. Feeling worn down, consumed by a need to love and be loved, I'd pray:

*I open my heart to you, Dream Woman. Help this baby have good parents. Let them love it. Make my father love me when I go home. Give us the chance to start over again so I can be normal. Please, help me! Amen, Dream Woman.*

No Second Thoughts

16 December 1964 – Hartford, Connecticut

Intermittent belly pains woke me just as rose-yellow dawn crawled up the windows. Tolerating the cramps until mid-morning, I then packed a small bag and walked to the hospital. A dark-haired nurse settled me into a bed, pulled up the side rails, closed the curtain around me, and curtly said, "The doctor will be in shortly."

Shortly felt like an eternity. When Doctor Haggerty did arrive, he affirmed I was indeed in labor and that all was progressing normally.

By two o'clock in the afternoon, the contractions were so strong and hurt so much I stopped moaning through them and began screaming. The nurse's lips were drawn into a thin line of concern as she checked me again and then hurried out of the cubicle.

A voice in my head screamed, *I want my mommy!*

Swimming in an ocean of pain with waves of nausea rising and falling, I hollered, "Crap, this really hurts! I can't stand it anymore!" Fumbling for the nurse's call buzzer, I found my hands tied to the sides of the bed. *What the hell!*

A smiling redheaded nurse magically appeared at my bedside. She held a syringe and needle that looked to me the size of a railroad spike. "Honey, there's no need to be so loud and so crude. You're upsetting the other women."

Eyes needed wiping, nose blowing, but I couldn't reach them. "The hell with the other women. I'm in pain and you have me tied up? What's that?"

"It's scopolamine and morphine, dear. It might make you feel a bit fuzzy. That's why we have you secured. But don't you worry. You won't remember any of this later."

*Later?* How the hell did I not notice being tied up *now?*

She was right about the fuzziness. Soon everything appeared weird. Shapes were distorted and a sensation of falling into oblivion, as if they'd taken the floor away, overcame me. I desperately clutched at the handrails trying to break my fall and keep from disappearing forever. Ceiling tiles went past my line of sight: one, two, three, four.

Now blotchy brown stains hovered over me and a green curtain surrounded me. Slowly reality dawned. Sliding my hands down my belly, relief infiltrated every cell as I explored the emptiness. An ache between my legs brought a smile. It was over. Sleep overtook me again.

A soft, gentle male voice called. "Carol. Carol, can you hear me? Wake up!"

Doctor Haggerty. I gazed in his direction, my eyes questioning.

"Everything went well. You're doing fine. You had a healthy boy. He's in the nursery now. Would you like to see him?"

"See him? Is that allowed?" This wasn't part of the plan.

"Of course you can see him. You can hold and feed him if you like. It will be three or four days before the social worker processes the paperwork for placement in a foster home. You will have those three days to be with him."

"You know my decision. We've been over this before. But...yes, I would like to hold him for a bit."

"That's good. I'll be back to see you later today and the social worker will be in this afternoon."

Never having asked about this part of the process, I'd imagined once the baby was delivered that would be it. Like any other hospital patient I'd recover, gather my clothes, and leave. I was fine with that. But having carried this child for nine months, the last few of which were very active—him kicking around and making his presence known like an insistent itch that simply refused to stop—I certainly was curious. But it never occurred to me they'd allow me to see and hold him. How strange. Was this perhaps a trick? Maybe they were trying to scam me into changing my mind, into keeping him. After all they didn't have an adoptive family for him yet; maybe they couldn't find one. Or maybe this was a standard procedure so they could cut down on the incidence of seller's remorse in hysterical, young unwed mothers.

As the door opened and a nurse entered carrying a blanket that looked like a football entered, none of that mattered.

*He's in that blanket. Do I really want to do this? Should I do this?* Instinctively, I accepted the blanket with the baby wiggling within. He was pink, cute, and chubby-cheeked. A healthy one, weighing in at six pounds twelve ounces, the nurse told me. Encouraging me to feed and burp him, she gave me a bottle and asked if I needed her to show me how to hold him. Shaking my head, I thanked her and declined. I'd cared for Harry when he was a newborn so I had that part down pat. She brought him to me twice that day. This raised my suspicions even more—all this time they were allowing me with him, the intimacy of it.

If anything, holding him made me more stalwart in the belief I was doing the right thing for both of us. No second thoughts!

My only day with my baby boy was an emotional one.

"Hey, baby. Are you glad to be here?" He was cute, not too scrunched but with a small bruise on each side of his head from the forceps during delivery. He seemed to be happy. He didn't fuss or cry. Instead he just lay there looking at me, taking it all in. In fact he was quite sweet. "You are going to grow up to be handsome and strong with a wonderful, loving personality," I crooned.

Unwrapping him, fingering his tiny limbs, I spoke as if he were a little man who could understand everything, "Look at you with your ten fingers and ten toes, so pink and soft. You smell like talcum powder, and look at your hair. At least you have hair; all I had was peach fuzz when I was born." Stroking his soft hair I placed him on my chest, warm flesh to warm flesh feeling the weight of him on rather than in me, while a saline ocean flowed from my eyes, soaking both of us. Passersby might have thought me a little loony, perhaps still suffering from effects of the medications.

He seemed to listen intently, his eyes focused on my face, as I softly explained what must be done, that he would live with someone else, that I simply couldn't provide for him and desperately needed a fresh start. I went on to promise I'd see to it his new parents wouldn't hurt or evict him. That he'd have a good family, a solid family who would love and respect him for himself, meet his needs as he grew into the brilliant, accomplished young man I knew he would be.

When the nurse took him away for the night, my mind drifted to myriad topics, not the least of which was the impending final break of the tie with my child.

I'd been living in Hartford for two months subsisting purely on savings from the waitressing, sales, and secretarial jobs I'd held over the past year. Having eliminated frivolous spending from my budget, there was enough money for the studio apartment and for food to last until this was over. Arrangements for the doctor's and hospital bills were being handled by the social worker.

81

CAROL LILLIEQVIST WELSH

I had come up with the plan to reconcile with my parents. It would solve all my problems. My unsafe-sex mistake, which was maturely and magnanimously being taken care of—would be behind me in a few days. Now all that was left to do was give this baby away, crawl back to my parents, and start over again. Back in my old bedroom with a rent-free roof over my head and a hot meal awaiting me every night, everything would be fine again.

Untruths

17 December 1964 - Hartford, Connecticut

The next afternoon a social worker from the
adoption agency came to the hospital and escorted me
to a small room away from the nursery where, choosing
a seat with a view, I glanced out the only window,
folded my hands in my lap in an attempt to control my
anxiety, and waited, jiggling my left leg while she dug in
her large briefcase.

Finally she plopped a mountain of papers on the
Formica-covered table: her missions to explain the
adoption procedure, offer counseling, and complete the
necessary ton of paperwork. I found myself distancing,
rotely answering a myriad of probing questions,
pretending to be more mature and composed than I felt,
just getting through the ordeal. Signing the papers, I
told more lies. In the boxes on the birth certificate sheet
where they asked for information about the baby's
father I inserted ancestral information about my former
fiancé. This was part of my fabricated plan, to give my
baby something better—not shame him any more than
my irresponsible actions already had.

In my mind this baby wouldn't grow up with the
label "bastard." He'd have something to be proud of,
not an unknown background. Unfortunately it never
occurred to me that falsifying the documents might have
an effect on him or his identity. I was too self-centered,
young, and wounded to think that far into the future for
someone else.

The social worker listened to my experiences of
growing up with my adoptive parents and what had

83

brought me to this point. I'd made a promise to this baby. So reversing our roles, I pressed her for answers. How selective would the agency be in placing him? Would she take extra care to ensure phony first impressions didn't sway their thinking, that due diligence would be done to guarantee he wouldn't be treated the way I'd been?

But how could I really be sure she'd follow through? I doubted that I could, but still my urging was insistent, sincere, and hopefully that would be enough.

She reassured me she would do her best and offered counseling which, in my withdrawn and determined state, I vehemently declined.

My other indiscretion that day happened when one line on the relinquishment form took me by surprise. "It says here, baby's name. Why would I be the one to name the baby? Wouldn't the adoptive parents do that?" I asked.

"The adoptive parents will most likely rename the baby, but until everything is official we don't like to just call him 'Baby' so we ask that you give him a temporary name."

Of course that was how it worked—my birthmother had named me Carol Ann and Glenn and Margaret hadn't changed it.

Pressed to come up with a name quickly under the watchful eye of the social worker, I wrote down "Glenn" as the first name followed by the name of my no-longer fiancé as a middle name.

Desperately wanting to put it all behind me, I named my baby after the man who'd beaten and thrown me out of the only home I'd ever known, shutting me out of his life, but who now offered a second chance.

Sabotaged

18 December 1964

Using the hospital solarium phone, my finger shook so much that I misdialed twice before getting it right. Nerves fired overtime, causing my knees to weaken and body to tremble as I waited for my mother to pick up. At the sound of her voice it took all of my inner strength and restraint not to blurt out, "Guess what? You're a grandmother!" I had to play this carefully so my plans wouldn't blow up in my face.

"Hello?"

"Hi, Mom, it's Carol," I said, taking a deep breath as I smiled into the phone, knowing she could sense my expression on the other end, setting the stage for a pleasant conversation.

"How could you *do* this to us? We know where you are and we know what's going on. Do you want to give him a heart attack? He doesn't want to see or hear from you *ever again*. Do not come here. You're not welcome!"

I got that feeling you get when you've stood up too fast, as if someone has turned down a dimmer switch that makes the world recede, where your knees weaken and you wonder if you are going to turn into a spineless pool on the floor. Sliding down the wall into a heap, I clutched at my belly. Not even on the night they threw me out did I feel such a metaphorical punch to the gut, such a hollow darkness. What had happened? My plan was perfect, followed to the letter: all I's dotted and T's crossed. What on earth happened since we had confirmed my homecoming earlier in the week?

CAROL LILLIEQVIST WELSH

An insurance person happened! While I was busy
signing away my son on the maternity floor, an office
clerk sitting in a cubicle in the bowels of the hospital
took it upon herself to call my parents for information
regarding payment of the bill. When they found out
what the treatment was for, a bomb exploded, bigger
than Nagasaki and Hiroshima combined.

But wait: the clerk called on a weekday during
business hours. How had my father found out? The
doctor and the social worker had readily agreed to keep
my condition and care confidential even though I was
under twenty-one and thus still considered a minor. The
floor nurses knew not to speak about me to anyone
other than the doctor and the social worker. *Mom must
have told him. Why couldn't she have called me first?* The
prison warden hadn't changed.

How could I have known to alert the billing
department? Fingers and toes grasped at every hole in
this crumbling dike; I'd missed one little breach and
now the floodwaters of disaster barreled over me.

Crying, wailing, I pleaded with my mother, "Please.
Can't you talk to him? Don't you care? I'm not keeping
the baby. You don't have to have anything to do with it!
I'll do anything you ask, follow all the rules and scrub
the floors, anything. Please, I need you, Mom!" I
sobbed.

Mother remained cold and resolute. Nothing fazed
her not even a plea from her first child.

"No! Your father doesn't want anything to do with
you. Don't darken our door ever again." She hung up.

If ever there was a time when I could have seriously
considered suicide this was it. But I was too full of raw,
exposed emotion, too within myself to formulate such a
plan. Those calls to my mother, my plans to return
home had been in vain. All they'd been were calls to a
cold, business-like secretary. Not once had Father's
voice graced my ears since that fateful night years
earlier. The best I'd been able to do was catch Mother

during the day while he was at work. A call in the evening, when he might have been around, would have resulted in "click" the moment he heard my voice.

Was it really *Dad* saying all that? Did he really hate me that much? Or was Mother being her manipulative, tattletale self?

Burying myself in the thin hospital bedcovers, I holed up the rest of the day and most of the next, shirking offers from the nurses for food and comfort, not talking because it was just too hard to say anything out loud.

I'd sure shown him, hadn't I?

And now it was over, all over. No family, no baby, no lover, no money, no job, and no self-esteem. My life felt like a whirlpool, a toilet being flushed—shitty no matter which way you looked at it.

CAROL LILLIEQVIST WELSH

A Low Point

The experience of giving birth and then
relinquishing my son provided a real-life lesson in
letting go. Not forgetting—just disempowering, letting it
be, and beginning the forgiving process. Forgiving
myself for past relationships, for getting pregnant, for
screwing up the chances of reconciliation with my
family.

Many years later a transformational quote by
Edward M. Hallowell in his book *Dare to Forgive*
expressed what I could only know by intuition at the
time.

"Forgiveness is so hard because it represents giving
up on the wish that the past will be different. Maybe the
greatest obstacle to forgiveness is hope. As long as you
are hoping the past will change, you can be angry that it
hasn't." I could no longer hang my hat on the anger of
the past.

19 December 1964

I left the hospital, the baby, and my past,
returned to a warehouse suite in Hartford, and crawled
into bed once again. Hugging my teddy bear I stared out
those big-paned windows bawling my heart out, weeping
for both my son and myself. I sobbed into exhaustion,
and then cried some more right through the most
miserable Christmas of my life. Bah, humbug!

After the holidays, the social worker visited as
scheduled. Again she pushed counseling and asked so
many questions that I became impatient. Explaining that
papers would have to be signed later on to finalize the

88

adoption, she wanted to be sure she could get in touch with me. "What are your plans now, Carol?"

The promise to my baby that he would have good parents would be kept. I wouldn't run off. I'd sign her papers and continue to bug her about finding good people for him. I had no intention of leaving either of them in the lurch.

However, I may as well have put fingers in my ears and sung "La, la, la, la, la" for all the attention I gave to her offers of counseling and help. Accepting anything like that would affirm and prolong my now-over-with pregnancy. How could I move on if constantly prodded to talk about it and be reminded of my shame, worthlessness, and nonexistence in the eyes of my no-longer parents? Like many girls in my situation, I disassociated from my emotions to block the pain.

One morning soon after the visit from the adoption worker, I quit pitying myself. Dream Woman had visited and inspired me during the night.

Everything that had been tossed my way provided a perversely exciting challenge. The innate fire deep within made me a brave adventurer. Who knew where it came from, but most certainly it was there. The time I spent wallowing in bed had been natural; to experience no pain, no sense of loss at all would have been almost pathological. Of course, I possessed the capacity to emote, to feel bad if the situation merited it. But more importantly, I had the ability to put it all aside when the moment passed and draw on that internal fire, moving forward with almost daredevil glee. Call it postpartum elation!

All my life I'd been a planner. To me, only someone programmed not to think for herself went through life without a plan, just putting one foot directionlessly in front of the other.

My Plan A at the time had been a good one. I'd relinquish the baby, reunite with my parents, go back to school, then get on with my life and a career. Plan A had also included reconnecting with Carolyn and Bill who showed me more love, support, and concern than my actual parents. Plan A had provided a sense of relief and new direction.

But then the insurance clerk had contacted Glenn.

Having gone through all the typical stages of grief and being worn down living these lies, I was ready to be done with all of that. Plan B needed activating.

My Hartford rental was paid through the end of the month but I was running out of money fast. Time to color outside the lines once again, make the quantum leap and get out of Connecticut. I would be flying solo.

A check up with the doctor assured I was fit to leave. Handing me a prescription for birth-control pills and telling me to keep frozen peas on my breasts for a few days, he wished me well.

I couldn't go home, but I did reach out to the Richardsons. They were delighted to hear from me and extended an invitation to spend the holidays with them.

Now six, Harry was excited to have me back, even if only for a week, and I lavished my attention on him. During our visit, Bill and Carolyn discussed my plans to move to Washington, D.C. and find a job. They were supportive and encouraging.

"If you can't find a job you can always come back and live with us again," Carolyn said, tucking two hundred dollars into my hand.

## Sowing Oats

Driving slowly south, I prayed the old car would make it all the way to the nation's capital and kept my teddy bear next to me, rubbing his worn skin with my fingers from time to time. Miles ticked off on the odometer as my anticipation for this new adventure grew and I focused on the future, nothing more. The first stop on the itinerary was Georgetown. While on a family vacation here not too many years earlier, I vaguely remembered my father saying something like, "You could consider attending college here" and "It's a nice part of the city. Safe, too."

Locating a coffee shop, I perused the newspaper, then stuffed coins into a nearby pay phone and began setting up job interviews and appointments to look at apartments.

That first night, the car was my home. I dozed, doors locked, all bundled up in just about everything I owned so I wouldn't freeze to death in the January cold.

The next day I fixed myself up as best I could in a nearby gas-station washroom for my first interview. Miraculously, two days later I'd managed to sneak in under the wire on a typing test and landed a position with AT&T as a secretary—something I'd never considered before as that was Margaret's venue. I was to start right away and I boldly asked for an advance, having spent all but a few dollars of Carolyn's money for rent on a modest apartment in Arlington, Virginia off Glebe Road. They gave me twenty dollars against my first check that would come in two weeks. The small studio apartment with secondhand furnishings suited me just fine. My new windows weren't as big as the ones in

91

Hartford, but the bed was comfortable and the toilet flushed. What more could I ask for? Living on lettuce salad and ten-cent boxes of macaroni and cheese made with water or the occasional bottle of milk stolen from unsuspecting neighbors' stoops, I scraped by that first month.

Nights are always hard when you're alone. Your mind tends to wander, forcing you to face reality on its own terms. I'd fidget around in bed, tossing and turning, wrestling with some dilemma, then somehow wake the next morning with an answer and satisfied resolve—an odd thing—as if a guardian angel in the form of my Dream Woman visited me, whispering to me in my sleep, telling me what to do. I learned to trust these intuitions. Some people dread mornings; I looked forward to and relished them.

The secretarial job lasted all of one month. I barely had the proper qualifications to begin with, although I'd already learned the street savvy way of knowing how to bullshit through a job interview: "Oh yes, sir. When employed with Mr. Rogers, I very capably handled several tasks at the same time. You can call and speak with him if you'd like."

The big downside with this AT&T job was how much the boss reminded me of Glenn—freckles, sandy greying hair, accusing look, and a faint smell of Old Spice. This was a bad demon that was best avoided. So I quit.

Broke again, I hit the pavement and happened upon a job at a florist shop, a good fit for both my employer and me. Having worked with flowers before, I felt at home among the sweet smell of blossoms and potting soil and didn't require a lot of training. This was a very busy shop, one of several that catered to the embassies and large functions of the wealthy. Using my creative talents, I arranged huge baskets of flowers for funerals and weddings, made bridal bouquets and corsages, all the trappings for bar mitzvahs, and soon became a valuable employee. With spring came an opportunity to work in the nursery department and here I learned more about plants and shrubs. I began to laugh again, liked my coworkers and was successfully making it on my own.

I'd recovered from the birth but hormones and loneliness still played havoc with me at times and, without much conscious awareness, I became involved romantically with an older married man.

Dating married men seemed to be a theme with me. It wasn't intentional and being married certainly wasn't a requisite for a date. But because they were father figures I could look up to for advice and comfort, I sought out older men. They were safe ground, didn't expect a commitment, and the illicitness of the relationship made it an exciting challenge.

It was a crazy time in my life. I was running from myself and toward myself all at the same time, figuring out who was the real me, and how to fit into this world—not unlike most young adults. I was a twenty-year-old girl in an adult body, and at the end of the day whether a man was in my life or not, I only had myself for support and advice. I'd made some big mistakes especially when it came to men.

Ending the florist relationship, I quickly moved on to another married man who raced sports cars on weekends. He taught me about cars and reminded me of my joy in the thrill of speed. I even entered a couple of powder-puff races.

While hanging around the racetracks, yet another married man came into my life. Was I allergic to single men, or was this a phase of that postpartum elation?

With each relationship I pushed the limits—only by doing so would it be clear if they could stay the course and truly love me and accept me as I was. Only then would it be safe for me to disclose my past. Self-defeating behavior since no one wants an abusive relationship, and now I was the abuser by acting impossible to love. I wanted Daddy, hated Daddy, wanted Daddy again, but wanted him to accept me on *my* terms, and then was only satisfied if those terms were nearly impossible. Apply, rinse, and repeat.

This new father figure in my life was a big-name drag racer and owned a "wheelie car," one that does tricks. Excitement, speed, and thrills were waiting for me with this new man.

I didn't have any ties to D.C., just as I didn't have ties to anywhere. I was a free spirit in a time of free-spiritedness. Hippies were doing their thing in Haight-Ashbury while my new man traveled the race car circuit. Why shouldn't I go where the wind blew me?

Trading the '49 Plymouth for a tiny Sunbeam Imp, the only thing my pocketbook could afford, I again packed my life into a vehicle and drove cross-country, headed for California, anxious to be reunited with the newest so-called love of my life.

Headlights cut through the blackness of the night like a beacon as the Imp climbed and then descended the mountainous terrain of Tennessee. Just before dawn, the transmission developed a glitch and kept slipping out of gear into neutral. I held it in gear with my right hand and drove with the left until I reached Memphis. There I purchased several yards of two-inch wide elastic at a five-and-dime store and, using Yankee ingenuity and a small amount of knowledge gained from watching guys work on race cars, looped it through the seatbelt bolt behind the driver's seat and then around the shift lever. At each town, or when going up and down hills, I'd unwrap the elastic and shift through the gears then wrap it back again to keep it in fourth until the next town or next hill. Amazingly, I made it to California in only four days.

Approaching Los Angeles and listening to "The Little Old Lady from Pasadena" on the radio, I felt intimidated by everyone whipping past me at breakneck speeds while I "Imped" along. Seeing a billboard advertising a flashy foreign car dealership at the next exit I impulsively pulled off the highway into the sales lot. Surprised at being given credit, I traded the Imp for an awesome navy blue Triumph Spitfire sports car. Now proudly cruising down the freeway just like the Little Old Lady, too fast for my own good, I thought: how groovy! A spitfire car for a spitfire girl.

Later that morning I hooked up with Ed. We spent a month in California before starting the next race season traveling around with his mechanic from drag strip to drag strip. These racetracks were located in some of the most remote parts of this country, which gave me a chance to see a side of America totally different from the one where I'd spent my childhood.

While Ed was on the road, his wife held down the fort and family in Southern California. In her absence, my role was "road wife." Maybe she suspected our relationship, maybe she didn't.

We were like nomads—all very hippie and bohemian—life was good. A home with a white picket fence wasn't on my radar just then. Staying in motels around the country or when necessary, sleeping in the vehicles added more excitement to an already exciting lifestyle.

After the cross-country trip in the Imp, hanging out with these guys turned me into a female grease monkey. Pretty soon I was covered with grease and lying underneath a car. If a coal miner took my fancy, I would have been spending all my time underground, black as soot. I'd bloom where planted.

Never having been a "don't want to break a nail" girly-girl, the entire thing appealed to the tomboy in me. I prided myself on my appearance and carried myself with style as I'd been trained, but at the same time I didn't mind getting dirty nor did I take any shit from anybody, male or female. When faced with a conflict, my first impulse was definitely not to slither off to buy a pint of ice cream and gossip about it on the phone with a girlfriend. I stood my ground and spit fire.

Freedom and adventure! I felt sorry for those Stepford-wives-in-training left behind in Connecticut, their lives already all planned out. *Unadventurous, boring plans*! They might have loving families, but for a time in all people's lives they should be young and free. I'd met too many people along the way who'd woken up "middle-aged crazy" because they hadn't ever gotten this stuff out of their systems when young and single.

Granted, if I'd had my druthers, I would have waited until after college to exercise my freedom. But that wasn't an option.

Some of Ed's features were similar to those of my father; sandy-haired and freckled, he even acted like him at times (his good side, not the abusive one). Was I acting out some subconscious Electra complex in choosing males who looked like my father? Was the desire to be loved by my father what drove me toward a certain man? Once the whole déjà vu aspect became clear, I'd bolt.

Ed and I agreed to part when the racing circuit season finished so when we arrived back in California, he went home to his wife.

Ed's mechanic Nick was now free to come courting. The three of us had spent a lot of time together on the road and knew each other pretty well. While Ed was often busy with publicity stuff, Nick and I would be together working on or taking care of the car. We'd grown to be close friends and now decided to move to an apartment together in El Monte, a suburb of Los Angeles. Nick moonlighted as a movie stuntman when he was not working with Ed, and I searched for and then landed another secretarial job. Life was good again!

On a whim while driving past a used car dealer one afternoon, I picked up a black Cadillac hearse for an incredibly small amount of money. Nick had done some side work for a talented designer who modified vehicles for movies and, just for the fun of it, he helped me trick out the hearse—my own Munster's coach. It was a blast going to drive-in movies in it.

Nick and I shared a lot of good times and enjoyed being together and having a more normal life. I'd grown tired of hopping from one married man to the next and hoped this relationship would lead to something serious, something more permanent. But over the next several months instead of exploding a relationship with destructive, testing behavior, I imploded it by killing Nick with love and a desire for commitment, pushing too hard and too fast for marriage. The result? Nick moved home to his mother.

Once again, I'd screwed up.

1965 - 1968

## Dancin' and Cruisin'

In response to the breakup, I rebelled by quitting the secretarial job. Taking another risk I found a great paying job at a bar in town as a go-go dancer. This was a time when "go-go dancer" did not mean "stripper" or "porn star." Goldie Hawn was a go-go dancer in real life too then, which got her on *Laugh-In*, where she played among other things...a go-go dancer. We wore skimpy bikinis and knee-high shiny leather boots, dancing in cages or on stages. Partly protection from groping hands and partly a good marketing ploy, nevertheless the cage thing was a little weird.

Although I loved to dance and had once fantasized about being a Rockette, the attraction to the job was the travel. Just like racecar drivers, dancers worked a circuit. I'd dance one place for a night or two or three, then a booking agent would call and let me know where to go next. It could be twenty-five miles down the road or halfway across the country.

Unable to afford the apartment on my own any longer, my hearse provided cheap accommodation and strangely enough, offered an ominous sense of security. Who would bother someone sleeping in a hearse?

I traveled all over the West and Midwest living in the hearse, towing my little sports car behind me. I was my own style of hippie!

Pretty soon what started out as a little local California thing had me sitting somewhere in Nebraska. Sometimes a show would finish at one or two o'clock in the morning, and then I'd be on the road all night headed for the next gig. Again Yankee ingenuity came in handy, like traveling with a big empty bottle with a

funnel attached to avoid having to make "pit stops."
Pity the person following too close.

As I drove through little one-horse towns I'd see
open mouths and surprised looks on townsfolk when
they saw the blonde chick behind the wheel. If only they
knew I was a go-go dancer going off to work in some
biker bar!

Everywhere I went, just like the guys in *Easy Rider,*
I ran into every flavor of hippie, dippy, yippy, and
groupie. The American counterculture was in full
bloom. It was funny how many runaways were out
there—how many rebels without causes. Many did have
significant causes like protesting the war and marching
for civil rights, women's rights, and gay rights, but a lot
simply decided to drop out and see the world.

Occasionally I'd meet real people of the road who
were older, but more commonly found myself rubbing
shoulders with other boys and girls like myself—kids in
their late teens and early twenties trying to "find
themselves" and discover "the real America" and make a
change in it for the better.

The drug scene was at its apex but drugs just
weren't my kick. I'd tried pot a few times and found it
nauseating. As for all the other stuff—such as
hallucinogens—those too held no interest for me.
Alcohol was my drug of choice. Occasionally, I would
do some sort of upper in order to stay awake while
driving hundreds of miles after a show but that was
more of a trucker thing than a hippie thing, for safety
rather than recreation.

I escaped simply by escaping. Maybe if I'd still been
living under my parents' roof in Connecticut where it
would have been easy to get drugs and people routinely
looked the other way, I'd have been taking stuff like that
by the fistful just to tolerate the situation. But if the
goal was to journey and have an adventure, well, I was
doing that and having a lot of fun along the way. I lived
without fear, moving forward, driven by determination

and wanderlust—*following a fire within.* My hearse and I were layin' rubber to the road, while stoners were just sitting under a tree somewhere, going nowhere outside of their own imaginations.

After a while, the grueling schedule and dancing in front of ill-behaved men led to burn out. Yes, a piece of the burn out was also self-loathing, thinking of myself in the way that Glenn had labeled me—nothing but tits and ass—and I was ready to raise myself up and become respectable once again.

Stopping in Amarillo, Texas I rented a small house on a quiet street in a quiet neighborhood on the outskirts of town and found a job as a hostess in a restaurant with a nightclub. Parking the hearse in my back yard, I settled down.

For company, I rescued a white female Pekingese from a dog pound and named her "Little Bit" as she was small enough to sleep in a shoebox. Other than myself, she was the first being for whom I took responsibility. That dog went everywhere with me—the car, into bed, into the grocery store stuffed in my purse. She was a friend and confidante with whom I shared bottled-up thoughts and feelings. Even if I had wanted to see a counselor, it was out of my price range—a luxury of my past. As for the new friends and lovers along the way, no need to talk to them about my past. Why should I? That was none of their business. Sure, a lot of us chewed the fat about the families we'd left behind, but that was common ground among rebellious teens out on their own. Abuse, pregnancy, and giving up a baby for adoption, well, that was different. I didn't want to be judged, nor did I wish to be pitied or shamed. So Little Bit got an earful.

When I'd left the Richardsons, almost a year and a half before, we'd agreed that we'd keep in touch. I'd promised to inform them of my whereabouts and activities. We usually talked on the phone every three weeks or so on a Sunday.

One particular Sunday, Carolyn gave me disturbing news. "Carol, I have something to tell you that might be upsetting. The McCallums went to court last week to legally disown you."

"You're *kidding* me! What, were they afraid I'd lay claim to one of their precious antiques or something?"

"I'm sorry, Carol, try not to let it bother you. *We* love you and you're always welcome here."

"Yes. You and Bill have always been more like parents to me than they ever were." After hanging up, I yelled, *Assholes!*

I might not have bled when the knife went in, but that night lying in the darkness with the conversation replaying over and over in my head, the blade twisting in my imagination, I felt as if I would hemorrhage to death.

After that, time stood still in Amarillo. I worked, paid bills, had a roof over my head, a vehicle, food for Little Bit and me, and was around people I liked—living purely in the moment. At night it got dark; in the morning, the sun came up. Those were the only things that mattered.

I was living the celibate life so it took me by surprise when I met George. We established an understanding right from the start that allowed our relationship to work very well: neither of us wanted a long-term commitment.

Pollyanna

4 December 1967, Amarillo, Texas

Relaxing on the sofa with Little Bit while waiting
for George to come home from work the phone rang. It
was Carolyn.

"Hi, Carol. Happy Birthday!"

During our monthly calls Carolyn would frequently
say something that had a profound impact on me,
shaping my thoughts and life. I opened up to her easily,
although I'd never told her about the pregnancy.
Outside of that one secret, she was a confidante. She
knew pretty much everything that was on my mind and
she supported the sowing of my wild oats. She neither
degraded nor judged instead she gently encouraged me
to think about my future. I needed someone like her—
an adult figure who really knew me, liked me, and
promoted a good sense of self.

"Thank you. What a nice surprise. We talked just
last week. How are you?"

"Going crazy. There's a client with huge IRS
problems that I'm trying to sort out, and then there's
the usual preparations for the holidays. Wish there was
more time in a day. But how are you? Do you have big
plans for your birthday?"

"I'm good, just relaxing here with Little Bit havin'
some girl time, before George gets home. He's taking
me out to eat tonight to celebrate, but we won't be late
since I have to work the early shift tomorrow."

"What are your plans for Christmas?"

"George and I thought we'd buy a tree and have
our first Christmas at home together. I've got some time

105

off 'cause the restaurant's closed for five days. The owner is going away with his family. It'd be nice if it would snow though, brown grass doesn't seem right at this time of year. What's Christmas without snow, right?"

"How would you like to spend Christmas with us in Connecticut?"

"Really? Oh, how I'd love to." I replied, as my mind planned. Then shaking my head, disappointment in my voice, I went on, "I don't have any extra money right now and George and I agreed we'd spend Christmas together, so I guess I have to say no."

"Well, what if George came with you? We'll buy your tickets. Consider it your present. There's a flight from Amarillo that will get you in to White Plains at a decent time on the twenty-third. I'll pick you up."

My planning mind blanked. *Wow!*

Carolyn broke the silence. "Tell you what, talk it over with George and I'll call you tomorrow. We love you, Carol. Happy birthday."

*How incredible!*

Perhaps if Carolyn had approached me earlier on in my adventures, I'd have declined her invitation. But time had passed and the heart-tugger of all heart-tuggers was an invitation for the winter holidays. Not Thanksgiving or Groundhog Day but *Christmas and New Year's!* Here was a family who really wanted me, asked me to come home. Talk about your Christmas miracles.

Carolyn, Bill, and Harry were delighted when we accepted their offer.

Thoughts whirled. I'd be going back to the scene of the crime so to speak. I'd successfully relegated Glenn, Margaret, and Ginny to the far recesses of my mind until Carolyn told me about them going to court, now I would again be in their backyard. Would curiosity get the better of me? Make me drive past their door and give them the finger?

Carolyn picked us up at the airport chatting all the way home, making George feel more comfortable right away. "We're so glad you could join us."

Harry was excited, happy to see me and delighted to have someone who would play guy stuff with him, as he and George got down on the floor with a host of action figures soon after we arrived. Christmas morning Harry was up early, snooping around the tree and soon we were all sleepily sharing in his joy, sipping coffee as we opened presents. Carolyn outdid herself planning and preparing a spectacular dinner. It was a true family event.

The next day Carolyn and Bill asked us to join them in the living room surprising the hell out of me when they said, "We've all talked it over and want you to officially become our daughter. We would go to court with you and change your name to ours—an adoption of sorts."

For the second time in a month I was left speechless, my mouth hanging open. This time, instead of having a strangled chicken feeling in my throat, I felt overwhelming joy. It would be official. I'd have a family. I'd get a second chance at being a daughter with a mother and father who loved me unconditionally. All I could manage in response was a smile as I wiped away tears.

"This will affect you, too, George. We expect Carol to move back here and go to college. Why don't the two of you go for a walk and talk things over?" Carolyn prompted.

We walked alongside the stone wall bordering the lagoon, stopping every so often while I gazed at my reflection in the still water. George encouraged me, saying, "This is a miracle. You have to do it! This could turn your whole life around. You deserve this, and they obviously want to give you that chance you've been looking for."

Later that afternoon I accepted their offer. That evening we celebrated by opening a bottle of champagne and toasting "To Harry's big sister."

I would be expected to help around the house, transport Harry back and forth to his private school in Greenwich, assist with his schoolwork—as some academic challenges required tutoring—and also help him do eye exercises for a vision problem. But there was a catch. While Harry was in school each day, my task was to figure out what kind of respectable career piqued my interest and to which schools I wanted to apply. *College at last.*

The morning we were to leave, I borrowed the car and drove George around town showing him Tod's Point Beach, my elementary and junior high schools, and the house I grew up in. I was shocked to discover the McCallums had moved. Carolyn hadn't mentioned that. As it turned out, they had bought a larger house in the more prestigious countryside of Greenwich. Now their going to court made more sense. Living in rural Greenwich, they could profess to have only one daughter. Their neighbors would never know they'd swept the other one under the carpet. They could have their picture-perfect family and fit in.

George and I focused on our separate futures during the flight to Amarillo. No hard feelings, no regrets. We wished only the best for each other.

Selling the hearse and my few pieces of furniture, Little Bit and I pointed the Spitfire toward Connecticut.

The next few months with Carolyn, Bill, and Harry were a wonderful adjustment. Harry enjoyed, and sometimes tolerated, having an older sister who spent time with him, took him cool places, helped him get his homework done, and fondly tousled his hair. For me, having a younger brother was a welcome novelty. Watching over Harry was a true joy and privilege.

While Carolyn and Bill kept busy with their separate law practices, I comfortably settled into the new role.

My wandering heart had had its fill of on-the-road adventures and my self-image was ready to begin its rehabilitation. I felt as though I'd stepped into a nice hot shower, washing away my teen pregnancy, go-go-dancing nights, and days of chasing married father-figure men. All those remnants of the road rinsed off and swirled down the drain at my feet. Now I had a clean slate with people who loved me.

But my dark secret gnawed away at my conscience. Even if it meant risking rejection, I wanted to come clean and tell Carolyn and Bill about the pregnancy.

1968 – 1973

Metamorphosis

Glenn and Margaret had disowned me. I had a new family, one who loved me despite everything they now knew about me.

March 1968

Bill and I stood before the Judge, elbow cloth to elbow cloth. Bill's confidence seeped though the fabric reassuring me, although my armpits prickled with sweat and my legs wobbled, feeling like they might collapse at any minute.

"Yes, Sir. No, Sir. Thank you, your Magistrate," I mouthed, just as "Dad" and I had rehearsed.

Done! In a matter of minutes, I had a new identity.

My youth ended at age sixteen and I'd been out on my own for six years. Now at twenty-two I'd been given another chance at life—a Pollyanna do-over that made me feel like Little Orphan Annie adopted by Daddy Warbucks.

My bedroom was across the hall from Harry's on the back of our three-story fieldstone house. Carolyn and Bill's bedroom was over the large living room with its wide French doors that opened onto a porch. Both rooms had a view of the lagoon and the rustic-red, wooden footbridge guarding the lower sluice end that emptied into Long Island Sound.

Bill loved sailing, as did Ted—their close friend, neighbor, and Carolyn's business partner. We all belonged to the local yacht club. Their love of wind, water, and boats meant we spent a lot of free time sailing. My brother was a good sailor too, and he and Bill sailed in club regattas all summer, then ice boated in the winter. Once I went ice boating with them. They had a funny ritual for keeping warm on these excursions. Putting on wool long johns, they'd get in the shower wetting them with hot water before donning oilskin foul-weather gear. I preferred summer sailing.

Harry didn't like doing homework or eye exercises but buckled down under my tutelage and began to improve in school. Sometimes we'd do something "grown-up" on the weekend. Once I took him for a ride in a small airplane. The pilot flew low over our house delighting him and his friend Matt. Several times we went to sports car races. Harry thought his big sister was pretty cool.

Life was good for my furry friend Bit, and me, in our new home. That is until one day when at the town beach, sand scrunching through our toes as we ran, a large Weimaraner snatched Little Bit in its mouth, shaking her back and forth as if playing with a stuffed toy. Screaming, I wrestled with the dog until it let go of Bit. Her neck was broken, life taken from her instantly. Hugging her warm, still body close to mine, I ran as fast as my trembling legs would take me to my car.

Shaking from head to toe with anger and sadness, hardly able to see through my tears, I somehow drove home, her dead weight pressing into my lap and my broken heart. Dad came running at the insistent blaring of the car horn. Holding both of us in his arms, he comforted me until I stopped crying, and then together we buried Little Bit in our back yard.

Opposite our house on the other side of the lagoon stood a big green Victorian house with many gables, which was rented by six airline pilots, that they'd nicknamed "The Island." Back in the '60s, we knew no more swingin' a job than being a jet pilot for a major airline. Those guys were like rock stars. The "mansion pilots" hosted frequent parties and invited Dad and me over many times as Bill loved music and was a talented drummer.

The pilots' parties were not riotous drug-filled orgies, but classy gatherings often with good food, music, and dancing.

Summers we'd be out on their beach roasting pigs or water-skiing with guest pilots, stewardesses, and friends from their own and other airlines.

At one of the Island parties, I met a nurse from England. Olivia and I hit it off instantly. Finding a quiet corner in the roomy mansion, we struck up an intimate conversation and, in spite of barely knowing each other, exchanged histories. "My husband was killed by an out-of-control lorry (truck) soon after our wedding. He'd only gone to the corner grocer."

"I gave up a child for adoption."

Olivia's nursing schedule in England allowed for blocks of four days off at a time, and with her stewardess girlfriends' ability to get free or cheap airfare, Olivia came to the pilots' house fairly frequently affording us the opportunity to become close friends. During one jam session, Dad introduced her to a musician friend of his. The two of them instantly fell head-over-heels in love—and he was married. (See how much we had in common?) Theirs became a wild and tumultuous international romance!

On a more serious side at home, Carolyn would make me sort through brochures and information on schools, weighing the pros and cons of different careers. I'd been a bright girl and a good student before my social troubles began. In high school I'd wanted to teach physical education or become a nurse—the cliché of the era; women were to be nurses, teachers and secretaries, while men were to be doctors, lawyers and captains of industry. The feminist movement might have started in the '60s, but it didn't really bloom until the '70s.

Being a lawyer, Carolyn was an exception to the rule. She was not only a tax attorney, setting up businesses for others and representing them with the Internal Revenue Service when needed, but she also played the stock market and was pretty good at it making money in hardware and software computer companies, among others.

She saw the future and, like the guy who kept saying *"Plastics!"* in the movie *The Graduate,* her mantra was computers. "You really should consider being a computer programmer. It's the future, Carol."

*But ugh!* The thought of math, circuit boards, and codes disgusted me.

I did however admire Carolyn for encouraging consideration of another perspective, and most certainly she'd seen the future with a clear eye. Had I followed her lead I might have been a Bill Gates.

As much as Carolyn wanted me to pursue computer programming, I leaned toward nursing and impressed her by doing considerable research into nursing schools.

At the end of April, while I filled out applications at the round Formica kitchen table, the doorbell rang. There was Ginny, slender, long blonde hair hanging loosely down her back and wearing a Cheshire Cat grin, her hand tucked under the arm of a tall, handsome young man in a blue sweater. Home from college, a bit more confident now, but still nervous—fearing being caught seeing me—she'd stopped by to proudly show off her engagement ring.

"Congratulations. What a surprise. Come in. Can you stay for a bit?" I said, after composing myself.

Settling in on the living room sofa, I encouraged her to talk of college and their wedding plans. We both intentionally avoided any discussion of her parents.

"I too have exciting news. My new name is Carol Ann Richardson. Carolyn and Bill adopted me in March." I could see from her wide eyes that she was as surprised by this as I was by her out-of-the-blue visit. Her fiancé hadn't said much, coming across as shy, but I could tell he really cared for Ginny even in the short time we spent together. As we all hugged goodbye she and I agreed to keep in touch.

Hearing Ginny's stories of college life, my interest in attending school gained a new fervor.

My internal fire strengthened me throughout the good and bad times. It helped me stand up to Glenn and his abuse; pushed me to finish high school while living out on my own; helped me relinquish a son for adoption. This flame had propelled me toward a life of fearless adventure as a young single woman on the road.

Now back home—albeit a different one—that spark ignited again, pushing me forward into the next chapter of my life, whatever that would bring.

CAROL LILLIEQVIST WELSH

Credibility

Carolyn took her role as a parent seriously, working to get me back on my feet into the real, more productive mainstream world, thinking like a career-minded person.

She pushed hard for her own alma mater. "Yale has a marvelous nursing school. You're bright. You won't have any problems getting in. If necessary, Dad and I can pull a few strings."

"Thanks for the vote of confidence. I'm considering a couple schools and I will look at Yale," I said. The deterring fact was that Yale was just too near Hartford for comfort.

"Look at all you've done with your life. You, of all people, shouldn't be afraid. I know you'll make a good decision."

While sitting on the pilots' beach soon after Ginny's unexpected visit and discussing what I should do with Olivia, she proposed, "Why not go to nursing school in England? You could stay with me when you were off so you wouldn't have to be in the dorms the whole time. The training is superb and it won't cost you anything other than your airfare to get there. English nurses pay no tuition and we're even given a monthly stipend."

Room and board—even laundry—was covered. I wouldn't have to incur any further debt to Carolyn and Bill, which would soothe my conscience since they had already done so much for me. *Why not go to England?*

London! What a mind-blower. To live in London at the height of the British Invasion—the Beatles, Carnaby Street, and the Mod scene—it would be totally groovy, baby!

The following week, with Olivia's help, I applied to a few nursing schools in London and several in the States, secretly hoping to be accepted by one of the English ones.

In June, Carolyn went with me to visit schools in Delaware, another in New York State, and of course, Yale. Actually, any of them would have been fine—and I'd have to make a decision soon—but my fingers were secretly crossed, wishing to hear from overseas.

Finally on the last day of June, St. George's Hospital conditionally accepted my application, pending an interview.

I spent the rest of the summer dreaming about living in England while I worked on preparing Harry for being on his own again.

I'd come to call Carolyn "Mother" and meant it from the deepest part of my heart. The time we'd spent living under the same roof was incredibly short and sporadic, but our bond was strong—stronger than mine had ever been with Margaret. So it was with pride and sadness that she put me on the plane for Europe so soon after having adopted me.

September 1968 – London, England

Olivia met me at Heathrow airport.

The next day, tired yet excited, I nervously checked my reflection in store windows as I hurried to catch the tube (underground rail) for Hyde Park Corner.

The interview went well and St. George's accepted me on the spot, placing me in the September class (known as a set) that would start in ten days.

After calling home, I celebrated by spontaneously trading my return ticket to New York for a round trip to Madrid and spent my last days of freedom attending a sports car race, a bullfight, and touring the Spanish countryside.

Returning to London, I bid Olivia adieu and moved into a dorm room in Knightsbridge. Dorm life was a big comedown from Carolyn and Bill's home, but it was no more Spartan than some of the accommodations I'd experienced on the road. Besides, Olivia's flat was available for escape whenever I needed.

Escape I did, for my room was a rectangular closet as sparsely furnished as a jail cell holding a smaller than twin size bed, a tiny study desk and chair, and a wardrobe barely big enough to hang four or five uniforms. The small window at the end of the rectangle provided a spectacular view of another brick building. The loo (bathroom), which six or eight of us shared, contained a shilling-eating metal box if one wanted hot water. Strange that they provided food but not hot water.

Hanging out in the common room where we gathered to avoid our closets, I learned a lot about friendship. These girls shared from the heart, envied and advised, yet weren't judgmental. We were all on the same team, competing for success in the world and not against each other. The prize was the coveted SRN (State Registered Nurse) and, if we did well, there were enough jobs for all of us. So we helped each other achieve our goal by studying together, reviewing, practicing taking one another's blood pressures and pulses, and rejoicing in our accomplishments. I'd never had girl-group camaraderie before and reveled in this new experience. In our free time, we window-shopped on the King's Road, chatted up guys in the pubs, or hung out in bistros, discussing the present and future. None of us had much money but, like all college kids, we found places and things to do that were affordable by pooling our hard-earned pence.

London felt like home, though I couldn't put my finger on why. It was as if I had some sort of inexplicable rooting there.

In the fall of my second year in nursing school, I moved out of the cramped dorm room into a cute King's Road flat with Olivia. King's Road was famous, a posh shopping and pubbing street where one might even see a *Beatle*. Our two large-paned windows overlooked the green manicured sports fields of the Chelsea Barracks. For our morning ritual, Olivia and I would hang over the window ledge sipping tea while watching the fit, sculpted young men of Her Royal Majesty's Special Forces (equivalent to the Green Berets) practice combat games and compete in soccer, often times with bare chests. What young woman in her early twenties wouldn't love to have had our flat?

Not having been home since school started, I'd earned a vacation. England was known for its fog and rainy weather and lived up to that reputation, so after a wonderful week long reunion with my parents and Harry, I headed for the sun and surf of Florida.

I'd heard that Ginny and her husband were living in Richmond. Finding her number in the phone book I called. She was happy to hear my voice, inviting me to drop by. I was surprised to learn she'd not married the fiancé I had met but a different boy, and that they had a little girl named Sandy. I was an aunt! Glenn and Margaret hadn't been happy with her decision, but had adjusted, and now looked forward to times with their granddaughter.

After two hours of catching up on each other's lives, keeping the conversation superficial, unsure of the sisterly bond between us, we hugged goodbye. Neither of us suspected it would be years before we'd see each other again.

Back home I discussed with Carolyn how it didn't seem fair—and how angry I felt—that Glenn and Margaret could accept Ginny's decisions and her baby, but reject me and mine. Her matter-of-fact advice calmed the fire. "I'm sure it hurts. But there's nothing you can do to change it, so let it go, Carol. Concentrate on nursing and your future instead."

I'd definitely made the right career decision. Not only was I learning new skills, I was having fun, feeling useful and appreciated. We were under a lot of pressure to take nursing and its responsibilities seriously, but some aspects of training could be lighthearted. A prim-and-proper British 'sister' (nurse manager) lectured one day, "Now, girls, you must always be professional. When on the medical ward, you may need to sniff flatulence or examine a patient's stool for it could be an indicator of a serious ailment." Soon my colleagues and I were holding our sides, stifling giggles.

Six months into training we rotated onto the night shift. Here, I took my responsibilities more seriously as one of only two nurses on duty. I would wrap my thick, navy wool peacoat cape around me, feeling the soft long-john-red-flannel lining warm against my skin as I made rounds from bed to bed, carefully watching for the rise and fall of sleeping chests, willing myself to stay awake until the littlest slice of dawn seeped under the large ward windows, bringing the promise of a new day. By the time bolts of liquid yellow flooded the ward, the meds had been dispensed, pillows fluffed, and patients were sitting up ready for the day nurses to begin their routines. I felt reenergized, satisfied, and accomplished by having seen my charges safely though the darkness of night.

For almost a year—until Olivia's musician guy finally asked her to marry him—she and I were roommates. But when she married, I too relocated, finding a more affordable flat with a small yard closer to the hospital.

In nursing school we were surrounded by doctors both young and old. *No more auto mechanics or rodeo clowns.* The interns and residents were as poor as we nurses, but we still managed good times and fine dates.

Among many dates I had two serious relationships. One I'd hoped would lead to marriage and boldly asked him to share my flat, which he did. Six months later, wanting a dog, we moved to a houseboat on the Thames—still no white picket fence for me. Aquatic living was fun and romantic—especially when I was bobbing to sleep at night—though it also had its disadvantages. Our yellow Lab had a thing for beer. Slipping her collar, she would go to the pub at the end of the boat dock, lap an unsuspecting patron's pint then saunter home, smelling of Guinness and lager. Of course if *you* sipped a pint too many, you could end up in the drink before making it to bed. One time a body floated past as we ate on the aft deck, spoiling our dinner.

Even though an ocean separated me from Carolyn, Bill, and Harry, we kept in relatively close touch and I could tell something was amiss from Carolyn's short letters.

During a springtime visit home, it became obvious that Carolyn and Bill were struggling with their marriage. Both had challenging law practices that kept them working long hours. Carolyn was traveling to New York City with her work partner Ted, often staying overnight, while Bill took on more of the household management and care of Harry. Neither of them spoke more than a few words to each other during my whole visit as they ran their conversations through Harry or me. I returned to London with a heavy heart.

By the time my friend Cathie and I returned home to visit that Christmas, they had divorced.

Carolyn married Ted, her business partner, the next year. (I later learned it was Ted who had been instrumental in bringing me back from Amarillo several years earlier.) Ted's home was at the other end of the lagoon and that's where Cathie and I celebrated Christmas.

Cathie, Harry, and I spent Boxing Day with Dad and his new wife. I'd been a little nervous about the new arrangement but both days turned out to be fun as we sledded, made snowmen, and just relaxed.

One of Cathie's wishes was to see the nation's capital. Donning backpacks, we hitchhiked to Washington D.C., saving what little money we had for food and lodging. Our first ride took us all the way to the last rest area of the New Jersey Turnpike before a storm moved in. Standing on the side of the road with sleet pelting our faces and wetting our clothes, we decided to walk back to the rest stop and purchase two large black trash bags that we converted into raincoats by cutting holes for our heads, leaving a slit for a hitching thumb to stick out. Not long after, someone took pity on the two pitiful looking trolls and gave us a lift all the way to our destination. Having found a YMCA for the night, we set out the next morning to see the city. Our cabbie drove us through Arlington Cemetery and insisted on showing us where the "noisses" killed in WWII were buried. He liked our British accents and we laughed at his Brooklyn one.

After graduating from nursing school, I bid farewell to my boyfriend and our floating flat as I chose to add certification in Obstetrics Nursing by taking a course at a hospital in Portsmouth on the south coast of England with a couple of friends from St. George's. Here, helping women birth their babies with a better understanding of the physiology and pain of childbirth, I began to view my own experience of years before from a new perspective.

Nurses in England didn't earn a lot of money, even with extra certifications. The government's philosophy was that since they paid for our training we owed them a low salary in return. Not that nursing was extremely lucrative anywhere at that time, but the pay in Britain didn't correlate to the amount of training we'd received.

I was surprised to discover that hospitals from other countries were anxious to offer us positions. Recruiters came along. Our reputation was well known;

British-trained nurses were some of the best in the world. My, it was nice to be validated!

A recruiter from Dallas, Texas gave a convincing presentation one evening. Their offer sounded like the best deal on earth. "Your starting salary will be ten-dollars an hour. We'll pay for moving expenses and plane tickets, as well as cover the cost of housing for the first three months." (In England our monthly stipend was the equivalent of forty-five dollars.)

My colleague, Christine, desperately wanted to sign up yet felt trepidation over being alone that far away from home. Seeking me out she asked, "Will you go to Dallas with me? Please? I'm afraid to go by myself." Such an attitude was completely foreign to me. I'd enjoyed five wonderful years in Great Britain and could easily have spent the rest of my life there, but the offer was enticing and I did miss my family.

"Let's put on our spurs and head for cowboy country!"

CAROL LILLIEQVIST WELSH

Unrest

1972 –1973 – Houston to Boston

Great job offers are often not as great as they
initially sound. Christine and I worked harder and had
more responsibility than the graduate American nurses
with their four-year BSN degrees (Bachelor of Science in
Nursing). Although we both had RN after our names,
foreign nurses were paid less, supposedly because we
were trained in three years instead of four. So much for
being the best and most sought-after nurses in the
world!

What we found was a lack of confidence and the
authority for decision-making in the American nurses
and often Christine and I would have to bail the BSNs
out of situations.

Christine and I'd been classmates in nursing school
but hadn't shared a living space in the past. Now living
together in an apartment, we discovered many
differences of opinion. Life in the same space became
strained beyond tolerance. Little held me there so I
chose to follow my desire and moved closer to the water
landing in Houston.

In 1973 the country was in flux. Gasoline was in
short supply due to an embargo precipitated by the
Mideast oil crisis that forced people to line up for hours
at gas pumps. President Nixon came under
congressional scrutiny while they investigated his role in
the cover-up of illegal behavior at the Watergate office
complex in Washington.

Houston offered a new non-hospital nursing
opportunity when I took a job as a visiting nurse.

126

As I pulled up in front of my patient's house, a group of black teenage boys surrounded the car. The taller boy came around and opened the door for me. "Hey, Nursey. Gimme your bag," he said, helping me out of the car and escorting me through the front door of his family's single-story row house. While I spent the next hour changing his grandfather's catheter and dressings, the other boys "watched over" my vehicle.

The grey-haired octogenarian was more interested in what was happening on the television in Washington than he was in what I was there to teach him about his diabetes and self-care. According to him that was his daughters' and granddaughters' responsibility—to care for him in his senior years. Several of his offspring were crowded together this morning, absorbed in the news just as he was, all of them already sweating in the humid Houston heat. It was if I were a fly buzzing around their heads disturbing their concentration. After finally getting their attention and finishing my tasks, I moved on to other houses where similar scenes filled my day.

I liked interacting with my patients and learning about a culture different from mine but the heat and humidity of southeastern Texas nearly drove me insane. At any given moment I was sure I could look down and find mold growing somewhere on my body. Cooler New England was more to my liking, more like England.

Olivia and I had kept in close touch while I lived in Texas. She and her husband were living in Massachusetts with their two-year-old son and she was pregnant with a second child. "Carol, if you're not happy there, leave," she said. "Come stay with us. There's plenty of room and I'd love to have someone to talk to while Frank is away all week working with The Boston Pops at Tanglewood. Just come!"

"All right, you've convinced me. I'll give my notice and be there as soon as I can."

127

After stopping home for a short visit with Mom, Ted, and Harry in Connecticut I joined Olivia and her family in Boston.

Cambridge City Hospital advertised an opening for a surgical recovery room nurse. This would be a new venue, but I was always up for a new challenge so I applied and got the job. Although it took a bit of adjustment for me to settle into the operating routine, I did.

Harvard Square, Faneuil Hall, the museums, and Old North Church—site of Paul Revere's famous lanterns—all of this and a small-town feel in a major American city. Dancing almost every night in disco clubs that had sprung up everywhere provided exercise and a social life. I dated often, but without commitment.

Boston reminded me of London with its brick townhouses, pubs on many corners, boaters on the river, and faces of many colors and cultures.

And though comfortable in Cambridge, fitting in here wasn't the same as it had been in England: an emotional connection was missing. Perhaps it was that Olivia had hurriedly moved, yet again, when her husband took a job in London only two months after I'd arrived, or maybe it was that so far, I hadn't made any good friends. But soon my thoughts turned to Jolly Old England, I longed for days gone by.

After six months of this nagging unrest the idea of returning to England and applying for British citizenship flooded my consciousness. Impulsively, I booked a two-week trip later that spring and made plans to stay with Olivia again. Perhaps I would be happier back on the other side of the pond.

1974 - 1980

## Squaring

John was an assistant administrator at a local city hospital and, for as much as people preach about the dangers of a workplace romance, neither of us paid much attention. We'd met at a hospital function hosted at the Boston Aquarium shortly after I'd booked my spring trip and, from that point on, dated exclusively. Initially, it was my accent that attracted him, wondering about the "cute British chick" he saw working in Recovery. Comfortable with the accent I'd easily acquired in England, I couldn't see any reason to leave it across the Atlantic especially as it allowed me an untarnished and mysterious identity.

John's sandy red hair, freckles, and impish grin attracted me at first, but soon I discovered a dry-humored, philosophical, and wonderfully caring man who was easy to talk to and willingly shared his own history of relationships gone wrong. In turn, I felt comfortable sharing my married man, hippie life days with him.

Our diverse conversations ranged from politics and medical practice to growing tomatoes and designer furniture. Saturdays would find us window shopping in Harvard Square, tucked between stacks in the Coop bookstore, or walking along the Charles River. John had an artistic eye for design, specifically as it related to furniture, and Cambridge housed several talented designers, but Charles Webb was his favorite. This meant a trip to Webb's studio at least once a month. John would run his fingers over the smooth finishes— not only feeling the craftsmanship, but the years of rain, snow, and sun that had grown the stately oaks Webb's creative works came from—and he'd dream of the day he could afford his favorite pieces.

On the other hand, I loved to dance. Our compromise for shopping all day was discoing at night. John wasn't as excited about dancing as I was but he humored me.

Although he might not have caused my knees to buckle or made me want to drag him into bed without a word, I welcomed his gentle, exploring touch that landed us there anyway.

He was the first man with whom I felt safe enough to open up and honestly share everything, facts as well as emotions—a major step in my ability to trust and commit to a relationship. With him, I began to chip away at the protective, ironclad wall surrounding me.

Sharing the initial reason for my trip to England, John expressed disappointment at my going and feared our relationship might end, but rallied with a positive attitude and showed his support by taking me to the airport, waving goodbye, and promising to pick me up in two weeks.

Olivia's telephone rang the following day. "I miss you already," was John's message.

By the end of the first week he'd called so many times asking me to come back that my thoughts of staying in England waned. Could this be the love of my life? Would I risk throwing it away by moving back here? When the plane took off from Heathrow at the end of the vacation, I was on it.

Within a year, we became so enamored with each other it cost me my job! Well, sort of. Even though I didn't report to him directly, as the administrator, we had concerns over being accused of nepotism, so I quit and found a position in an OB/GYN office instead. This move would eventually lead to an obstetrics career.

After an appropriate courtship period, I moved into his much larger and nicer apartment close to his oldest sister and her husband. John spent a lot of time with his sister and brother-in-law and socializing with them often allowed me an easy integration into his family. Having spent some time with street-smart people as well as some who were not so smart, I found John's family's classic intellectualism somewhat intimidating, challenging, and very pleasant. John's father had retired from Harvard after forty-two years as a marine biology professor, while his mother had graduated from Radcliffe. And although I didn't go to Smith or Oberlin, as their daughters had, everyone treated me as an equal, no one lording their schooling over me. Whatever direction the conversation took when in their company, I always learned something new.

9 September 1975 - Tuesday evening, Cambridge

John and I'd been up to Boothbay, Maine to see his parents for Labor Day weekend and our first day back at work had been hectic. While cleaning up the dinner dishes, we were discussing John senior and Martha's old-fashionedness. They were putting pressure on him to get married, particularly since they'd found out we were living together. Habitually smoothing his eyebrow with his left ring finger John said, "I wish they wouldn't push so hard. My mother just can't leave it alone, can she?"

Turning to face him with one hand on my hip and the other flicking the dishtowel over my shoulder I blurted, "Well, we could do something about it so they'd get off your back."

"All right then. Will you marry me?"

"Seriously?"

"Yes! Will you marry me?" he asked again, pulling me close and pressing his soft lips to mine.

My whole face lit up as I said, "Well, yes, I will!"

Wanting to please Pop and Martha but not wanting a huge expensive affair, we picked Columbus Day

133

weekend as the date. That gave us only six weeks from proposal to wedding day. With help from his sister, we somehow orchestrated a wonderful event.

One evening, while brainstorming the guest list, I reflected on my sister Ginny. Perhaps I wanted to prove to Glenn, through her, that his label no longer fit a successful professional nurse and soon-to-be wife—the ultimate opposite of what he'd accused me of being the day he'd thrown me out. I'd worked hard to let go of my "parents" after Carolyn's good advice, but wasn't sure how I felt about my sister. We hadn't kept our promise of keeping in touch. If she were willing, here was an opportunity to offer a hand in sisterhood for an adult relationship. Obtaining her address from Nan's mother, I sent an invitation, but our wedding day arrived and went without a response.

Someone else crossed my mind too. Now, from a comatose place within, I wanted him to know he needn't be ashamed of his mother; rather, that she was someone he could be proud of. This too, I would have to leave to a higher power.

John knew about the baby. It wouldn't have been right to marry and leave him in the dark about that. I'd told him some time after returning from England and he'd wrapped me in his arms—quelling fears of rejection—and accepted it as matter of fact.

Neither of us were virgins when we married and though I'd led a far more colorful life, John didn't judge. He loved me for who I was, even with my shortcomings.

25 October 1975

As puffy white clouds raced across a bright blue sky on a crisp autumn day, family and friends gathered on the front lawn of John's family homestead in Boothbay, Maine. The vibrant red and yellow maple leaves provided a picturesque background for our minister. Tightly holding the soft hand of my husband-to-be, happily awaiting the start to the rest of my life, I gazed around the circle of family and friends, momentarily reflecting on each person: Nan, my lifelong friend, horseshoe crab tormenting buddy, and now maid-of-honor; Andy, her jovial, opinionated husband standing with their two children; Carolyn—Mom—proud and beautiful with her coal-black-dyed hair and bright brown eyes teary with love; brother Harry growing out of his gangly teen years, becoming a man, so handsome in a suit; tall Ted, solidly loyal friend, supporter, and advocate; and Dad, the man who'd taken on a stray, protected me years ago, who now miraculously floated me across the grassy aisle as his new wife happily looked on.

John's folks and siblings stood to our left with their families. Many good friends completed the circle. After reading our self-composed vows, the minister's words drifted on the breeze like soft background music while I seemed to float above the ground as if carried aloft by the wind. John firmly squeezed my hand, abruptly bringing me down to earth just in time. "I now pronounce you husband and wife."

Guitarist Rick Charette played "Morning Has Broken," a children's hymn set to new music and popularized by Cat Stevens, as we expressed our love and gratitude to all six of our parents by handing them roses. We then made our way around the circle hugging and thanking each guest. An all-weekend celebration now moved into full swing with a clambake, cider-pressing, story-sharing, and an impromptu band made up of talented members from both families.

The first six months of our marriage were an unexpected adjustment. Having lived together before marriage our new roles caught us off guard. It is said that marriage changes a relationship and indeed it does—not for better or worse, but for both.

By winter we were settled enough to splurge on a delayed honeymoon to Bermuda. During the vacation, a career move for John occupied the center of conversation. He had reached the top of the ladder in his present workplace. A job change would probably entail moving from the Boston area. I had a great job with an HMO (Health Maintenance Organization) but, as a new wife readily deferred, and encouraged him to put out feelers. I would go wherever the wind blew us.

Several weeks later out of the blue John got a call from a college buddy who was CEO of a large hospital in Oklahoma City. He'd been looking for a good right-hand man and wanted someone he knew and could count on. Was John interested?

Brian needed John in Oklahoma by early June. I reluctantly stayed behind to tie up loose ends with my patients, transition my replacement in the practice, and pack.

God, I missed John. But keeping busy made time pass and I looked forward to our nightly chats on the phone. July fourth was bittersweet. Disappointed to be missing Boston's bicentennial events—particularly the tall ships parade in Boston Harbor, I was also excited to finally be joining my husband for our new life on the prairie.

Oklahoma

Oklahoma was not the total culture shock for me that it was for John. However, according to Oklahoma law, I was a foreigner. A foreigner? I had received my nursing training in that strange faraway land of Great Britain and the Oklahoma authorities weren't sure I could speak *English* even though by then my accent was totally re-Americanized.

"You're actually requiring me to take an English proficiency exam before I can apply for a license in this state even though I'm currently licensed in Massachusetts and Texas and went to school K-12 in Connecticut?" I asked, mouth agape.

Until the licensing snafu could be straightened out, I played hausfrau—a new role for me. I rather liked being a non-working woman for a change and really enjoyed playing with flowers again and growing vegetables. But mental boredom soon set in. Enrolling in an H&R Block course, I learned new skills that stimulated my brain and complemented my digging in the rusty red dirt.

Finally, the Oklahoma Licensing Board granted my license and I snagged a position in the maternity department of the local hospital. Four months later, I celebrated by getting pregnant.

I hadn't any qualms about *ever* being a mother. Margaret had been a poor role model, but Carolyn was a fine one. Giving up my first baby had been necessary and now, at age thirty-one, I was forced to think about that again. But all I felt was the familiarity of the physical state. I knew these stirrings of pregnancy, all

137

the changes my body would go through. Along with my acquired nursing knowledge there was the sense-memory of it, but I was emotionally devoid of anything concerning that part of my past.

I wanted this baby with John. I loved John. Loved my life. This was my next adventure. I had no regrets over a decision made years before.

Now married to a loving man, I was soon to be a *better*-than-wonderful mother, and was exactly where I needed to be to raise this baby in a home full of love, with everything he or she would ever need to grow up strong in body, mind, and spirit. This time I was ready.

Excited and proud, living purely in the moment, I welcomed each and every butterfly movement. Love for my husband grew as we celebrated our life together and the one growing inside. Unlike last time, I even gave up smoking the day the line in the little window turned color, never to light up again.

On Halloween, at seven months my belly stuck straight out. Wearing a cut-off T-shirt with a gigantic smiley face markered on my tummy, pretending my now outie navel was a nose, we went out trick-or-treating. This was "proud pregnant-woman" advertising personified.

John V

14 December 1977 - Edmond, Oklahoma

An entire week and a half of contractions did not make me a happy woman. There are names for these things—Braxton-Hicks, false alarms—but all they were was an irritant. When you're uncomfortable but not likely to produce results—a baby—within any reasonable amount of time, it is simply frustrating.

For my birthday John took me to the National Rodeo Championships in Oklahoma City. Whether it was the excitement of seeing cowboys and bulls or climbing to the top of the bleachers, mild cramps became contractions, regular and painful. They came so hard and close that we thought John might have to do a delivery on the way home—disappointingly, before we could contact the doctor they subsided. I was still pregnant.

Ten days later a pesky backache and the same mild cramping interrupted my routine all day long; excitement would build and then...no, not yet. We had company for dinner and with the main course of pasta consumed, everyone was well sated except me—I just wasn't hungry.

Staring at a growing puddle of warm liquid on the linoleum floor (a hostessing faux pas rarely described in *Good Housekeeping* magazine), I calmly stated from the kitchen, "Um, my water broke." Like a giddy schoolgirl I wanted to jump up and down but the good nurse in me said, "No."

Soon stronger contractions commanded attention. I'd tolerated them for a while, continuing to present the meal and socialize, but now unable to breathe through them any longer, I reached for John's hand and announced, "It's time! We need to go to the hospital."

"Oh. Oh! Okay." His hands shook, but bravely putting on his administrator's hat, he feigned calm.

"This is it, honey," I said, patting his knee as he sped to the hospital.

Excitement and anxiety coursed in my veins. I'd be sharing what can often be a rather humbling human experience with the people I saw each and every day. Good Godfrey, there's nothing like being in a buttocks-revealing hospital gown, legs spread-eagled for the world to see, then having to go back to work with these same people a short time later knowing they'd seen more of me than I'd like. Oh well, so much for modesty!

In 1977, identifying ultrasounds were not common practice, so we had no idea of the sex of our baby. John was the fourth John Henry in his family, and if we were to have a boy he would be named John Henry the Fifth. Oh Lord, quite a handle for a little baby to live up to, and some days that made me wish for a girl! Otherwise I didn't care as long as it was healthy.

There's an irony to being a birth coach then giving birth yourself. Even though we'd gone to classes, navigating our way through the process of becoming parents as equal partners, as a labor-delivery nurse and a certified Lamaze instructor, I'd unconsciously placed more pressure on myself as the expert and understandably John deferred to me. We both wanted this to be a perfect delivery experience without unrealistic expectations that could foster a sense of failure.

We felt better prepared than most couples, but labor was rougher than expected and I found myself on hands and knees, rocking back and forth in bed, attempting to control the pain and a growing scream by moaning, "Dream Woman, Dream Woman" and praying she'd help me find my misplaced peacefulness. Two hours later my nurse checked me again stating, "You're only four centimeters dilated." Shit! Surely I was further along than that considering all the pain. I continued to moan and rock.

While in the bathroom around 11:15 I nearly had an accidental water birth. An uncontrollable urge to push made me scream, "John, the baby's coming!" The baby was indeed crowning. Show time!

Scooping me off the toilet John hurried down the hallway toward the delivery room hollering, "Help, I need help, we're havin' a baby!"

Things went quickly. Our son John the Fifth arrived at 23:23 on December 14. Weighing in at seven pounds, six ounces he entered this world on his paternal grandmother's birthday. He would be called John V or JV, pronounced Jay Five, and naturally, Johnny.

Nature didn't allow me to contemplate the issues of raising a boy with a number after his name right then because a complication with the placenta arose, requiring immediate surgery.

Regaining consciousness hours later, I looked down at a perfectly formed blonde-haired boy with a turned-up nose. An overwhelming love aura surrounded us. As he suckled at the breast I felt him pull on my heartstrings, binding us forever.

New Business

Spending my days playing with, teaching, and watching over John Five gave me immense pleasure. Summers in Oklahoma can be unbearably hot for long periods of time, so hot you really could fry an egg on the sidewalk in less than a minute. I longed for the cool coastal breezes of Maine. John agreed it would be beneficial for everyone if Johnny and I spent the summer near his parents. They would enrich Johnny's life, provide opportunities for him to know them and to learn about the past as well as the present through their stories.

On the Boothbay property stood an empty rustic cabin, the perfect getaway that reminded me of GranMum and GranPop's Lake George home. It was a simple, natural place of peace and quiet with no phone—just what I needed.

It might sound like an odd arrangement, but it wasn't that unusual for many New Englanders to spend the summer away from their winter homes. Ever since John could recall, his family had summered in Maine with his paternal grandparents', while his father, having an academic schedule, would commute back and forth to Cambridge as needed.

This lifestyle supported the introspective, intuitive, and creative parts of me, and provided a spectacular place to parent a little boy where he and I shared quality time with few distractions.

John flew to Maine a couple of times during the summer and we wrote lots of letters—often the best communication—because one can say things in a letter that are not as beautifully said in person or on the telephone.

By the time John V turned one, I'd become antsy not having a job. Like a lot of women I wanted to do something outside the home, something mentally stimulating with adults, but I didn't want to go back to shift or full time work.

"John, what would you think if I started a business in health education? I could contract with hospitals to teach Lamaze classes. What they charge parents doesn't come close to covering the hospitals expenses, but without much overhead, it would give me a modest profit and I'd be doing something in my profession."

"That's a good idea," he said. "You already have an in with the Edmond hospital."

Before long I was self-employed, fulfilling the other part of my high school dream by discovering how much I enjoyed teaching.

Working evenings allowed me to lovingly focus my days on JV. I was proud of owning a business: no bosses to answer to, no punching someone else's timecard, but most importantly, the flexibility in my hours allowed me to do both jobs well—mothering and entrepreneur.

Marrying into this educated family who accepted my idiosyncrasies and faults and with a hardworking, supportive husband I'd staved off total *Stepford* wifedom. What would my next challenge be? Something between Wilderness Woman and Lady Cabot.

CAROL LILLIEQVIST WELSH

Blanchard's Camp

Summer 1979 - Boothbay, Maine

To get to our rustic cabin, we had to go by boat on a high tide or trudge a long twenty minutes through the woods. No running water or electricity brought out the self-sufficient, problem-solver, outdoors woman in me.

The official name for our cabin was Blanchard's Camp—titled for a friend of John's grandfather, a veteran of both World Wars. The wooden structure of shiplap boards—rough-cut true two-by-three studs set two foot on center—had nine windows, twelve panes in each, and afforded a view both up and down the Cross River. When there in the summer we removed all the shutters and replaced them with these windows; closing up for winter, the process was reversed.

Spending time in the woods in a rustic cabin can activate the Thoreau in any of us. We become one with our environment, noticing things we rarely see and enjoying the pleasures of simple tasks.

Most of what I learned about wood and construction was though watching and participating in the care of the cabin. Over the years, the place needed more and more work and, out of necessity, we now added a bunkhouse, which was an adventure unto itself.

Consulting with John's father—fondly dubbed Pop—we discussed how to build and attach new construction to the old cabin. Pop provided milled lumber from his property, while we hired two young builders open to the challenge of using hand tools and floating supplies on a raft over to the camp.

144

After assembling our supplies, we waited for a noon high tide. Early that morning, at "hard water" (the name Johnny gave to the mud visible at low tide), the men built the raft, then piled the supplies and a generator onto it. By noon, towing the raft with a motorboat, they'd reached the opposite peninsula, tied off close to shore, and waited for the tide to recede so we could form a people chain handing supplies up the steep embankment. A fun and muddy day!

JV woke us the next morning around six yelling, "Mommy, *men!*" in his loud four-year-old voice, jumping up and down, pointing at the river.

Wanting to help with every aspect of the project, I had to watch him constantly to keep him out of harm's way and not under the workers' feet.

Amazingly, it took only five days to finish the addition. I watched intently, totally captivated as the structure went up, studying the details of its construction.

With the bunkroom finished and the carpenters gone, taking their compressor with them, I went to work with our hand tools building bunk beds for JV and his cousins, and a queen-sized Murphy-style bed for John and me. So pleased with my accomplishments, I tackled a wooden countertop, a built in sink and a three-burner cook top for the kitchen. Just like GranPop McCallum, I'd discovered working with wood was good for the soul—and a practical and enjoyable pastime.

As John Five grew older, we made up stories and worked together on arts and crafts projects. We hiked the surrounding hills, boated, and played—bonding as a parent and child ought to. John V gained a respect for the environment and a healthy love for the planet. He would not be destined to spend his life in a climate-controlled cubicle and think that was the world.

During those cabin days, no longer the businesswoman, and rarely a wife, I was a mother, focusing solely on JV, and on making things right with myself. Subconsciously I was squaring with the child I'd relinquished and a past of abuse: coming into a new identity. Determined to let actions speak louder than words, those Maine summer days were my proving ground.

As time went by, ambitions for the camp increased and I turned it into a real summer home, laying pipe from the freshwater spring to the cabin for "running" water, creating an outdoor shower with a large plastic-lined bag with holes, and enlarging the front stoop giving us a place to play, above the often damp ground. Finding satisfaction in reading how to do something, then creating it, I became quite handy tackling things most women wouldn't even attempt, and making the place more habitable with little John Five at my side, a constant helper and playmate. I became so comfortable working with tools that I even made him a suit-of-armor out of roof flashing so he could act out his fantasies of being a knight in shining armor rescuing the damsel in distress (me), killing off dragons and bad knights with his duct-tape sword.

1980 - 1984

## Always Happy, Never Content

John did well in his new position and after four years an opportunity to be CEO of his own hospital and director of a building renovation project surfaced. Good news for his self-esteem and career, as well as for our pocketbook.

The hospital was located in a small town at the entrance of the Oklahoma Panhandle, smack in the middle of nowhere, albeit during a local oil boom. Luckily John married me, and not a more typical New England administrator's wife who might have shunned the idea of living in so remote a place. But I could be happy in Oklahoma or a cabin in the woods, and would easily adapt to just about anything so long as love and adventure were involved.

I became active in John V's preschool and soon contracted with the hospital to provide Lamaze classes. It came to my attention that unprotected sex was common in rural Oklahoma, resulting in a high rate of adolescent pregnancy. Concerned, I trained as a Straight Talk® facilitator through Planned Parenthood® offering a program that reached out to teens. The irony abounds. Was this a way to practice acts of kindness or perhaps pay things forward?

In life people frequently say, "I know how you feel," but how often is that really true? We surmise we know how someone feels but we rarely know from firsthand experience. In this particular instance however, I *did* know. I *had* walked in their shoes. Looking into the eyes of those young girls I identified with their situation, and approached them with sincerity and an open, empathetic heart. Maybe seeing the raw

149

honesty and determination in my eyes was what made "New Beginnings"—befitting the situation—so successful. Many young, pregnant, and unwed girls thought this was the end of the road in so many ways, but there I was, living proof that life, dreams, and futures didn't have to come to a crashing end in the face of adversity.

Teaching sex-education classes, I counseled girls on birth control and discussed options for when those lessons were ignored, or when luck simply wasn't in their corner.

As the business grew, Health Education Services seemed a more all-encompassing title, so I hired employees to teach the Lamaze classes which allowed me to focus on New Beginnings, networking with other businesswomen, and devoting time to John V.

Late that spring, the family accompanied me for a working vacation to a nursing conference in Colorado. Nursing in the United States was in transition. Nursing schools and workplaces were putting a greater emphasis on having a BSN degree (Bachelor of Science in Nursing) and phasing out the three-year R.N. diploma programs. Many nurses were encouraged to return to school to obtain the prized degree.

Grasping the benefits that credentials would afford me, as we drove back to Oklahoma I said, "Honey, I think I should get a degree. It would open doors and could help us financially."

Smiling, the little twinkle in his eye suggesting he'd known what I was thinking before I did, John methodically said, "I had a feeling this conference might stir you up. Go for it. You won't have any problem with schoolwork."

"Thanks for your vote of confidence I appreciate that. I'm just not sure what to get a degree in though. It seems redundant to go for a degree in nursing when I already have an R.N."

"Have you considered a related field instead?'

"Like what?"

"What about psychology?"

Jumping ahead, mentally already planning, I said, "I could easily change the days John V goes to preschool to match the days when classes are offered, but what about early mornings or a late class?"

"We could work that out. You should do this. You've talked about getting a degree before—now seems to be the right time."

Leaning across the car I kissed him on the cheek.

August 1980 - Alva, Oklahoma

Northwestern Oklahoma State University in Alva, Oklahoma was located twenty-five miles south of the Kansas border, eighty miles northeast of our home in Woodward.

The commute could be challenging. Some days the roads were uphill both ways (really). Oklahoma isn't all flat plains. There *are* hills there and I was traveling them thar hills two days a week. They gave little protection from gusty westerly winds. In summer, dust blew into every nook and cranny; in winter, snow drifted into huge whale shapes that could obstruct travel.

By studying psychology and sociology I was of course covertly beginning to understand myself—as in "physician, heal thyself." John had recognized my needs better than I.

Unfortunately I'd been out of nursing school too long to receive any credits toward a degree, and what credits could they give me anyway, having been "foreign" trained? So, I started at square one.

Successfully balancing my roles as wife, mother, businesswoman, and summertime frontier woman, I'd proved my abilities in multi-tasking. Now I added student to the list. *Just call me Wonder Woman.*

151

# CAROL LILLIEQVIST WELSH

## Lisa

### Summer 1982 – Woodward, Oklahoma

During summer break from school John V and I made our usual trip to Maine. My friend and neighbor, Gail, would row to Blanchard's Camp several times a week after work, or on weekends, to hang out with us. We'd sit on the rocks watching the tide ebb and flow, play with John V, discuss everything from apples to zebras, and attempt to solve all the world's problems along with some of our own. Gail's disappointment at not being able to have a child of her own came up frequently. She'd had severe endometriosis and an ectopic pregnancy making her chances of getting pregnant—or carrying a child to term if she did—slim to none. She and Doug had investigated adopting a child in Maine and found that disappointing as well. Too much red tape, and innumerable costs.

Through New Beginnings and my work with our local doctors, I was aware of several occasions when someone had privately adopted through an attorney and I thought I just might be in a position to help Gail and Doug. I offered to talk with our local doctor.

"You're serious? You'd really help us adopt?" Gail said.

"I'd love to have a hand in making you a mother. But I can't promise anything, Gail."

Rural doctors throuhout Oklahoma had an informal protocol and a network when it came to adoption. When one of them had a patient who wanted to relinquish a child they would activate the network, as people generally preferred not to put their babies up for adoption in the same town in which they lived. This professional courtesy among doctors allowed for a win-win situation for everyone involved.

14 November 1982

A female infant was born to an unwed mother in a central rural Oklahoma town early one morning. Her doctor called his colleague to say the baby had arrived and the mother was still committed to adoption. The baby would be discharged from the referring hospital about one hundred miles away within forty-eight hours. When Dr. Leo called me, I knew there was a lot to do in a short time!

At 10:00 A.M., I called Gail in Maine. She was at her insurance company desk shuffling papers. "Hi, Gail, it's Carol. I hope you are sitting down because you're the mother of a baby girl!"

After a very long silence she said, "A girl! A baby girl! Oh my God, I have a baby girl!" In the background, her colleagues cheered.

"What? When? Wait a minute. I've got to take my shoes off. Okay, tell me all the details," she said.

Relaying the facts of the birth as I knew them, I explained that the baby could only stay in the hospital for forty-eight hours from the time of birth. We needed to get things moving right away.

Gail shifted into high gear. "I'm on it. I've got my list started. I'll call you later. I need to go find Doug."

Later that day, Gail's disappointment and frustration was evident in her voice when she called me back. "We have to complete a home study before we can do anything and we're at the bottom of the list. This could take a while!"

I discussed the situation with John then called Gail back telling her we would act as foster parents for them no matter how long it took to sort things out.

To say the least Gail and Doug were ecstatic over becoming parents and named their little girl Lisa, proudly listening to her baby noises on the telephone. I don't know how they stood it being so far away for so long.

Lisa was our precious guest for six lovely weeks. Having a baby around again was sweet and as Johnny was now five he appreciated her without jealousy for all the attention she got. To him it was as if we were babysitting, or having a sleepover party with a baby.

Our four-member family had a nice symmetry. Like me, John and Johnny were excited with our new role. John V was good with Lisa, enjoying his short time playing the big brother—entertaining her, feeding, and even changing diapers.

I purposefully tried to avoid bonding with Lisa out of concern and respect for my friendship with Gail, and out of fear that long-repressed emotions might creep in. But unlike many foster-care families, we knew who this baby's parents were going to be, approximately how long it would be before they would take her home, and more importantly, that we would have a long-term relationship with her—which is not always the case.

Many years later Gail told me that Lisa imagined me as her "tummy-mummy." So bonding occurred one way or another, at least from her perspective. Of course Gail sorted her out.

But after having Lisa those six weeks, both John and I found it harder than we thought to send her home with Gail and Doug. This prompted discussions of another child of our own.

The aftermath of delivering John V left serious questions as to whether I'd be able to conceive again. And if we were lucky enough to do so, would the complications be worth the risk? We both had full plates with life swirling around us and so nothing came of our second-child discussions. That is until Christmas 1983.

## A Big Decision

John's renovation project for the hospital was winding down with an anticipated grand opening the following June. John V was enjoying kindergarten and excelled in all that was expected of him. I had entered my senior year at Northwestern Oklahoma State University, business was thriving, and life was good.

Christmas came and, as usual, we attended a number of hospital and medical-related holiday parties. Chatting with Leo, little Lisa's adoption doctor, I shared with him her first birthday photos.

"It's nice she's doing so well. Look at all that black hair. She looks healthy and happy. How are her parents?" he said.

"Good. They're really enjoying her."

"Are they ready for another child? I have a mother due in April who will be adopting out."

I shook my head, knowing for certain that Gail and Doug weren't in a position for another child at that time. But I said I would discuss it with them and then, on the spur of the moment, blurted, "Well, Leo, if you can't find anyone else to take the baby maybe John and I'd be interested." My tone may have been flippant but the idea had to have been lying dormant within.

Later that night over another heart-to-heart discussion with John, we agreed that adopting a baby would be a good thing for us. As much as I'd enjoyed my pregnancy and would have loved to carry another child, given my age and the complications I'd experienced with JV's delivery, the possibility of conceiving didn't bode well for us. We decided to sleep on it for a few days.

155

Mulling it over, and after talking with Leo again, we proposed the idea to Johnny. He'd enjoyed having Lisa around and the thought of sharing our life with another baby, one who would stay forever, excited him. What had started as nothing more than cocktail chatter suddenly turned into a plan.

Our birth mother was due to deliver in the middle of April. Time enough for us to talk to our attorney and so forth. By then I'd become even more of an adoption expert through counseling young girls and my trainning through Straight Talk®. It was like I'd been managing the Boston Red Sox and suddenly someone put a bat in my hand and said, "Now it's your turn to hit."

When I'd given up my baby in 1964 I hadn't been grilled for details. They'd believed what I'd told them and hadn't delved too deeply. The emphasis at the time had been on matching the baby's features and personality with those of adopting parents. This was a young white girl giving birth to a baby—enough said. However, that would not be the case when I was on the other side of the transaction.

Adoption practices had changed considerably over twenty years. Open adoption and single parenting were becoming common, and private adoption registries were springing up across the country, assisting birth parents and adoptees in finding each other. Many states were loosening their laws to allow disclosure of identifying information under certain circumstances.

As I saw it, my role was to advocate for the unborn child. From my nursing, psychology studies, experience with Lisa, and own intuition, I was sure later in life this child could face challenges requiring knowledge of his or her genetic make up, or that he or she might just become curious about their birth family. I wanted to be able to answer those questions as honestly and completely as possible. Without making the birth mother feel awkward or uncomfortable, certain questions should be asked. The more we knew, the better prepared we would be.

Beyond the mother and father's medical-social history I'd come up with an additional list of small details—favorite colors, clothes they liked, foods they hated, etc. This was serious business.

Pressing for an open adoption—which meant that the birthmother would know us and we her—I'd vowed to respect any wishes regarding contact.

The attorney who represented us as adoptive parents and as professionals was protective. Healthy, white, American newborns were the number-one request for adoption. That John and I would be getting one without any wait at all might be misconstrued as preferential treatment.

In an open adoption, the birthmother and her people would have discovered this. John was the face of the hospital in our small town. It couldn't appear that he'd stepped to the front of the adoption line while less fortunate folks had to wait. Right place, right time could be hard to explain.

Had our baby's mother also insisted on an open adoption, it might have knocked us out of the box if she had found us unacceptable as adoptive parents. But the open-adoption issue was mine, not hers.

Poor John. He was torn between trying to please his wife, self-appointed expert on adoption, and listening to his attorney on the possible effects an open adoption could have on his career. He spent many hours with folded hands, forefingers tented into a steeple, pressing them against his upper lip while deep in contemplation.

A compromise might be reached. Discussing my concerns with Leo, I'd proposed he pass me off as his office nurse. I could capture a first impression, imprint her image into my memory storing it for the future, and get my questions answered without her knowing I would be her baby's mother.

It was an impulsive plan that didn't fly. Our attorney hit the roof. "No way!" he said—no way would he allow me to glance at her even from across a crowded room. And as for my unrealistic list of questions, well, "Forget that, too." However, he did concede to asking a few. But, like Gretel, I did my best to leave as many breadcrumbs as possible along the way.

Lots of arrangements had to be made in order for us to pull off this adoption without any hitches. One of these was sorting out my final college semester. How was I going to fit a new baby into my already crazy schedule? I needed help.

Meeting with the sociology advisor, I took him completely into my confidence about the adoption. He arranged for me to transfer into night classes at an off-campus site closer to home. This meant only having to go to the main campus three or four times during the semester. He also arranged for an independent study class for the remainder of my credits. The task: thoroughly research and write the equivalent of a thesis on adoption that included my personal experiences.

Finding my true lineage, those genetic roots, now seemed imperative in order to fulfill the assignment. What goes around, comes around.

Laura

23 February 1984 – Woodward, Oklahoma

A baby in utero can't be reasoned with. We can try to plan for them but in the end they do as they please. This particular baby decided a February birthday was better than April and there was nothing anyone could do about it.

While stripping wallpaper in our bathroom, I was taken by surprise when John called from the hospital to say, "Our birthmother is in labor!"

"No! It's too early! This is only February."

Glancing at my watch, seven-forty in the evening, all kinds of concerns began to bubble into my consciousness. Ours was a rural hospital out in the panhandle of Oklahoma and this was about to be a premature delivery. In the best of circumstances we should have a pediatrician present, but the closest one was in Oklahoma City. I said, "Should we have Leo transfer her to a facility more able to handle a preemie?"

Although John covered the mouthpiece with his hand, I could hear him discussing it with the doctor.

"Here, talk with Leo," John said, handing the phone off.

"I don't think it'll be a problem. Her other two children were early and they did just fine. Remember she's a smoker," he said.

"But we aren't sure about her dates so we don't really know how preemie a baby we're dealing with," I countered. "What pediatrician do you use if we need one? And what about the nursing staff? How competent and comfortable are the nurses caring for a preemie? Do we have an incubator? Where do you transfer—Oak City or Enid?"

"Okay, since you're more comfortable with her being transferred I'll check her, see if she's dilating, then call you back."

Before he hung up, the loudspeaker in the background paged him to the delivery room...STAT! At 8:06 P.M. I became a mother for the third time. John called at 8:10 and in spite of his excitement, I could detect concern in his voice. "We have a girl. I saw her for a second, she's really tiny." Hearing worry in John's voice, I accurately imagined him bent over in his black leather office chair, pushed away from the desk, left hand on his head, right on his knee, a red-bearded dead ringer for *The Thinker*. "I'll have Leo call you just as soon as he's out of the delivery room."

At least ten phone calls went back and forth between us in the next hour. Finally unable to stand being alone any longer, John came home. Changing out of his suit into something more comfortable, he told JV and me all he knew about the delivery and the baby's condition, then gave both of us reassuring hugs before heading back to keep vigil and place a call to our attorney. God! I so wanted to go with him, to be in the nursery. I wanted to see our baby girl for myself and know she was all right, not be pacing at home trying to find patience and calm. I couldn't allow myself to relax, not just yet. This baby was premature. She weighed only five pounds. Things could go wrong. I worried just the same as if I had birthed her, feeling a responsibility toward the baby as if she were already ours. And I worried because she was a girl.

We'd wished for a girl—after all, we already had a boy and he would probably be our last biological child. But I worried because our birthmother had two other children, which we understood to be boys. Perhaps she would be more reluctant to relinquish a girl.

160

Soon absolute craziness began. Our attorney was skittish and concerned that someone would discover the hospital administrator and his wife were adopting a child by bypassing the usual red tape, concerned that people might talk of coercion—or worse—and he worried on our behalf that the birthmother might decide to keep the baby. He gave us strict instructions to maintain secrecy, at least until the mother and her family followed through with their plans to leave town. He didn't think it would be more than a couple of weeks. *An eternity when you're waiting!*

Adoptive families live on a razor's edge during the period after birth and before everything is finalized, where nothing is certain. Every nightmare is similar— the phone will ring and it will be someone informing you that you will not be getting a baby. For this reason most newborns are temporarily placed in foster care for the waiting period.

In an open adoption, the adoptive parents act as foster parents. Even though we weren't having an open adoption, we were to have this baby in our home soon after her birth. We were to act as foster parents just as we had for Lisa, but this time we wouldn't know if we were to give the baby back until the final papers were signed—a very different scenario from when we'd fostered Lisa. This situation was unusual in another way too—it was a secret.

More than anything I wanted to stay home and care for this baby myself, but that could have raised questions as to why I'd suddenly dropped out of sight. A good friend and nurse I'd worked with in Edmond, skilled at taking care of newborns, had agreed to play an important part in our undercover operation. She would accompany the attorney, receive the baby from the mother and secretly stay with us for a few days.

At the insistence of our attorney, I called "Grammy Jo" the morning after our new baby was born. Leo assured us that the mother did indeed want to relinquish and that the baby was doing well and could be released from the hospital later that day. During the six-hour round-trip drive to Oklahoma City I focused solely on the road, unwilling to allow my mind to play the "what if" game. Dropping Jo at the attorney's office around noon, I went home to wait with my "boys."

An hour later—after a circuitous drive around the outskirts of town to ensure they weren't spotted— Grammy Jo carried our daughter through the front door accompanied by our attorney.

"Oh, she's so tiny!" I cried, tears of joy sliding down my cheeks and wetting her forehead. "Is she all right? Did her mother get to hold her, Jo?"

Love and excitement filled us. The baby fussed insistently until her brother took her in his arms and she settled down, falling asleep.

Our attorney delivered a few words of caution. "Remember, you can't tell anyone that you have her for a few weeks, until the mother and her family leave town. And you have to name her by tomorrow."

"Tomorrow? She's only sixteen hours old and we just met her. How can we know who she is by tomorrow?" I countered.

We'd talked about naming her Sarah, from both sides of our families, but also felt it was important to consider what she brought to us: her uniqueness, personality, and a family history. Not knowing her birth family made it all the more difficult for us to name her. Of course, she would have our last name but her first name should reflect who she came from, her birth identity. It took over a week of getting to know her before we could decide (which made our attorney a daily pest). Finally we all agreed on the name Laura—our girl from the prairie.

Everyone was sworn to silence. Even JV wasn't able to tell anyone, which was tough on a kindergartner. I hated all the lies and secrets it reminded me of a pregnancy many years ago. I hated going about things that way but acquiesced and maintained silence.

Despite the encumbrance of not being allowed to let anyone know we had just adopted a baby, I was beside myself with joy, ecstatic to be a mom again.

Unfortunately, Laura didn't have a good first twenty-four hours, which took the wind out of my sails. Jo, too, felt uneasy.

*Not my new baby! No!*

Quickly my new-mom's hat came off to be replaced with a nurse's cap. That Laura was far earlier than the one month Leo had calculated was soon apparent. She shouldn't have been released to a private home, but should rather have been in a hospital skilled in neonatal care with pediatricians on hand.

I called Leo. "I'm worried about the baby. She's had several apnea attacks (stopped breathing) and is having difficulty feeding. She's unable to hold the nipple well and her suck is very weak. I think she's a lot younger than we thought."

"How long did she stop breathing?"

"A good sixty seconds. It took stimulation to bring her around, and scared me half to death."

"How is she now?"

"Better, I guess. She hasn't had an attack for several hours." Leo promised to stop over after he rounded at the hospital and before starting his day at the office.

While he checked Laura over, we discussed what to do and agreed on a plan. Given the secrecy issues, Jo and I would be vigilant for any deterioration in Laura's condition and he would make daily house calls. I should call if I became worried and, if need be, he'd get her admitted in Oklahoma City.

When we had decided to adopt at the end of December, I'd tried to re-lactate with the intent of breastfeeding the baby. Pumping several times a day for the last month, I was actually producing milk by the time Laura was born. But because her suck was poor, I now had to switch to a supplemental system, adding formula to the breast milk and feeding via a thin flexible tube attached to my breast. I kept her close to me, watching her hawk-like, just as I had my first patients in nursing school. Feedings improved slowly and by Sunday, when it was time for Jo to go home, we thought things were under control.

But during the next week she had more apneic episodes that continued to scare us. I couldn't take the worrying any longer and asked Leo to call the hospital in Oklahoma City to arrange to see a pediatrician. They confirmed my suspicions—estimating that, at birth, Laura was only thirty-four weeks and four days. Luckily—with good care, love, and patience—she did exceptionally well. But those first weeks were tentative and nerve wracking.

Taking someone into our confidence became necessary since going out to buy supplies would have been a *Mission Impossible*—at six, John V had long outgrown diapers, formula, pacifiers, and everything else a newborn needs. Our neighbor and good friend was a new mother herself and readily agreed to become our secret supplies agent. Without her help and support I'd have gone insane.

John and I also hired an older woman to come into our home to care for Laura on the QT. I spent as much time at home as possible but continued my regular routine—work, school, and John V.

Johnny loved his baby sister and was about to explode if he couldn't tell someone—anyone. We allowed him to pick one friend with whom he could share, someone we knew and could trust to keep the secret.

This was all quite strange. I sometimes wondered who was crankier—the newborn, the lawyer, or me.

A lawyer is supposed to ease the legal process but instead he made us feel like fugitives. And we were doing nothing wrong! This was a private adoption and had we been Sam the mechanic and his wife Laverne none of this would have needed to be handled in a clandestine way.

John and I had cut down on the number of social invitations we accepted but couldn't avoid all of them, so there I was, living like Clark Kent's Supermom disguised as a school-attending-housewife-PTA, business-owning mother.

During this bedlam, John managed quite by accident to see Laura's birthmother. "Please, please memorize every nuance of her features. If Laura should ever ask about her, we need to be able to describe her in detail." I even suggested hiring a police sketch artist to have him capture John's description of her image on paper while it was still bright in his memory. Unfortunately that never happened. One good thing came from his unplanned sighting though, John now realized we'd been misled—or had misunderstood—because Laura's birthmother had two little girls clinging to her legs when he saw her in line at the Post Office. *Fate?*

So many thoughts raced through my mind during those intense months. Selfishly I'd wanted Laura's birthmother to hurry up and move but, putting myself in her position, I couldn't help wondering how difficult it was for her. What had she told her family?

I held conversations with her in my head. *I promise to take good care of your baby, to treat her well. We'll love her for you and support her individual growth. I've walked in your shoes—our circumstances different: the results the same. I empathize with how hard it is for you to give this baby away: to make this decision.*

*Did you have the option of choosing us, or was that not presented you? Did you want to know more about us, too? Are you disassociating as I did? Distancing? Protecting yourself from hurt and shame? I hope you don't feel shameful, for you've given us a great gift. I promise to be as good a mother to Laura as you would have been.*

Fortunately, I didn't experience the emotional rollercoaster most adoptive mothers do—didn't question my parenting skills, as many first-time mothers do, or worry if this other woman's child would bond with us. But—different from most adoptive mothers—I was also subconsciously playing out what I'd hoped for my *first* son.

My love for Laura was instant. We shared the common bond of adoption. It's funny how often people will say an adopted child looks like their parents, and if that were the case, pride would fill me, but the only true resemblance was gender. Someday she would search my face, hoping to see her own reflection.

Toward the end of our fifth week with Laura, I was able to turn her fate over to my higher power, trusting that if we were meant to be her parents she would indeed be our gift. If not, well, we'd have been good foster parents—as painful as that might be for us.

I was so happy! But as I lay awake at night listening for the sound of Laura's breathing to change, indicating she'd finally fallen asleep, I couldn't help but wonder if her birthmother was lying awake, too.

Our luck changed in May when Laura's birthmother and her family finally moved. In sympathy for putting us through hell, our lawyer pulled some strings, rushing a home study and persuading the court to waive the standard waiting period. He arranged for the adoption paperwork to be filed early before the usual six months waiting period. Once finalized, Laura would be ours.

On May 30, 1984, I again stood before a magistate as Laura officially became our daughter.

John V celebrated by taking his baby sister to school for show and tell, finally announcing to the world we were a family of four!

Living the American dream with a husband, a career, and my children, I now had experienced all sides of adoption.

CAROL LILLIEQVIST WELSH

Out of the Mouths of Babes

When John V was about eight years old I faced another dilemma.

While I drove home from a fun outing at the Omniplex in Oklahoma City, he casually asked, "Mom, was I adopted?"

It never occurred to me that a biological child would have such a suspicion, particularly since we'd always been open and forthcoming about his birth, but he was a curious kid and though it was sort of ridiculous for him to suspect that we'd hidden such a thing, I had to respect his inquisitive mind.

"No, honey, you're all ours," I said, eyes crinkling at the edges as my cheeks rose with a smile.

Over the years we'd told him various anecdotes about his birth, such as the hard delivery and how, when he was placed on the scale to be weighed by his loving father, he greeted John by peeing on his chest. Every family has its personal legends and this one I now repeated to him, as he rarely tired of hearing it. He laughed as always.

"Why are you asking about adoption? Has it been on your mind?" I questioned.

"One of the kids at school says he's adopted."

Although recommendations on talking to children about adoption are abundant, little literature is available on when or how to tell your children that they have a sibling you gave away. At some point in my children's lives I knew I would need to broach this subject, but I hadn't practiced what to say.

His bringing up adoption made me think. *Should I tell him? Can he handle it?* I'd always been honest with him

168

answering his questions accurately. I decided he was old enough to learn that while he was indeed my natural child, he wasn't my *first* natural child.

"I have something personal about adoption to tell you that I haven't shared with very many people," I said cautiously, rehearsing in my head what to say next.

"What?"

Taking a deep breath I let it out slowly, then, "Well, you know I was adopted and my parents kicked me out of the house as a teenager, right?"

"Yeah, that was really stupid."

"Thank you for the vote of confidence, honey. After I was on my own, I got pregnant and at nineteen, I had a baby. We weren't married. It was during the Vietnam War and the father wasn't around to help me like your dad is. I didn't know how to take care of a baby when I was so young. I knew the best thing for both of us was to give him up for adoption, kind of like Laura was given to us."

His hazel eyes widened as he fell silent. Then he asked, "Does that mean I have a brother too?"

Amazing that at only eight years old he could put all that together so quickly. It took me by surprise. "Yes, I guess it does. But I don't know where he is or who he is—just like Laura's mother doesn't know about us."

"Oh," he said, before falling silent again. The way he folded his hands in a steeple tent like his father indicated he was still thinking about what I'd said, so I left it at that. If he wanted more, he'd ask.

The subject didn't come up again until high school when he referenced our conversation in a paper he wrote. He never seemed angry or judgmental of me. Perhaps because his sister was adopted, his understanding went deeper. If people who put babies up for adoption were bad then how would he have gotten his sister, Laura? Still, through the years he must have had the same passing curiosities I'd had. Did he ever

169

wonder where his brother was? What he looked like or how he was doing?

Once Laura was old enough to understand, I shared my story with her, too. Relating to the situation, she listened openly, aware she had two biological sisters she didn't know.

Still, something else churned deep inside me that needed to surface and be resolved: something that was missing. And a faceless woman I kept dreaming of.

1984 – 1998

Nailing Down

1984 – Western Oklahoma

"The child who is born into his family is like a
board that is nailed down from the start. But the
adoptive child, him the parents have to nail down,
otherwise he is like a loose board in mid-air," says H.
David Kirk in *Looking Back, Looking Forward* when
quoting an adoptee named Peter.
    Well, my parents never nailed me down, at least not
in any good way. A small piece of me was misplaced,
floating around in the universe untethered—always
seeking more.
    At times, I'd get a glimpse of that misplaced piece.
It would reveal itself through a dream, or as a gut-sense
intuition, but it was never quite close enough for me to
reach out and grasp. It kept me suspended in midair a
long time.
    Going through Laura's adoption opened anew the
door to my past. Now once and for all I felt I should
step through it and begin the process of nailing down.
    To do this I needed more details about my own
adoption and birth family. The issue was more about
getting information than finding any one person, for my
first parents were dead.
    The part of me that was a child and thought like a
child had accepted that. But now, reflecting with an
adult mind, I wondered: Was that a lie? Some sick thing
Glenn said to hurt me? Make me feel I had no other
options? That I was stuck with him and his rules? Had
he been elevating himself above the shame of infertility?
Or did I distort his words in my own mind, elevating

173

myself above the shame of illegitimacy, fantasizing an acceptable excuse for my relinquishment?

I hadn't thought of Glenn for a long time—but now, trying to reconnect with my true heritage, he once again rented space in my head.

My sister and I had been adopted through the Spence-Chapin Agency in New York City. Fortunately, they were still in business. Drafting a letter, I explained my plight. Their response was vague, little more than a form letter giving me broad platitudes. Describing my mother as unmarried and unaccompanied by my birth father, they provided a few more details, among them Swiss and Swedish nationalities—which surprised me as I had been told I came from Norwegian stock—but this was nothing I could sink my teeth into.

As I read this one-page letter, memories of the past jumped off the page. When giving away my child I'd made up stuff, manufacturing lies for the things I either didn't know or didn't want to be honest about, such as the truth about the birth father. Was this paper also just so much bullshit?

The last paragraph was all about how my mother hadn't really wanted to relinquish me but felt it was in my best interest. It described how she held and spent time with me in the few days before relinquishing me. I could only imagine that similar words had accompanied *my* son. Thus I was left wanting, disappointed, and confused.

Of course mine had not been an open adoption, so I wouldn't be allowed access to my birth parents' real names or addresses, just as my child could not get such information about me. It would have been easy to quit right there, but that simply wasn't my nature. The last option—and least favorable—was to bite the bullet and see if Margaret would be forthcoming with more information.

Glenn had died from a heart attack in 1978 and, with apologies to God, I'd felt nothing—nothing at all.

The last time I'd ever felt anything for the man was when I was going through my first pregnancy and needed to disengage emotionally from the impending relinquishment. Instead, I'd focused on the wish that he and Margaret would take me back into their home—a natural self-defense against a rather unnatural act. Hell, I'd even named my baby after him which spoke to my dissociative state.

Now that Glenn could no longer lord control over Margaret, hopefully she had mellowed and would be open to helping me. It was worth a try.

I discovered she was now living in Florida and considered picking up the phone or writing but was afraid she would ignore me. The best bet was to go through a neutral third party, our attorney. He drafted a professional letter informing Margaret of my research project relative to my ancestral history and asking if she knew the name of my natural mother and the state she was from.

Margaret's handwritten response was prompt and curt.

January 7, 1985
    Dear Mr. Harding:
        Due to frequent and extensive moves, Mr. McCallum and I, of necessity, eliminated many of our files rather than pack them once again. I have no information pertaining to the matter referred to in your letter to me dated December 28, 1984.
        Carol's action seems a strange turnabout for someone who always seemingly resented the initial rejection by her birth mother, and a rather sad and futile quest, instead of seeking and accepting the happiness that surrounded each of us in spite of some sadness and occasional disappointments.

175

> There will be no further communication
> necessary on this subject.
>                    Margaret McCallum (Mrs.
>                    W.G.)

*Stone cold!* Even after Glenn's death, she still continued his rejection of me. As a child in their care, I'd been tied to my bed and beaten, forced to eat my food off the floor like an animal, made to wet my pants rather than be allowed to use the bathroom, thrown out of the house, and officially disinherited. Yet, in her mind, this was the "happiness that surrounded each of us" and "occasional disappointments"? Was that really all I'd been to her? *My God!*

Rather than being defensive and angry, I knew on an intuitive level that forgiveness was the answer. *Forgive, forgive, and forgive. Don't let the past eat at you the way it has eaten her.*

I recalled Edward Hallowell's words from *Dare to Forgive*: "As long as you are hoping the past will change, you can be angry that it hasn't." Margaret just confirmed for me that the past wasn't going to change. I had to forgive and let go.

This would be the last communication of any sort with Margaret. Two years later, I learned she died of cancer.

Blind Search

Oklahoma 1985-1988

Laura's adoption was finalized the year I accepted a full-time job as the school nurse in Woodward. My responsibilities included administering and overseeing the standard school-nursing duties for three thousand students in eight buildings, as well as the task no one else wanted—sex education for grades five through twelve. This new job was on top of managing Health Education Services and mothering two children. One would think that would have been more than enough, but not for me. I now enrolled in Oklahoma University's advanced master's program, an advanced course offered in unique circumstances. Instead of regular classes on campus, the curriculum was mailed to students who then had six weeks to complete the course work before attending two full weekends on campus. On the last day, of the last weekend we took finals. It was a thirty-two-credit master's and I completed it in two years. In May of 1988, John and the kids proudly applauded as I walked across the stage to receive a Master of Science in Human Relations.

Thank God for summers in Maine where I played with the kids, relaxed by reading something other than course work, and enjoyed tranquility.

Then in fall of '85, with John's hospital renovations and construction project finally complete, he decided it was time for a career move if he were to continue upward mobility on the corporate ladder accepting a job as CEO of a rural hospital in the western mountains of Maine. This put us only two hours away from his folks,

close enough for all of us to be happy. My family were
six hours away, but after the remoteness of Oklahoma it
seemed like next door. John and I found a small three-
bedroom house in Dixfield just a short ten-minute
commute to the hospital—a nice place for our kids to
grow up.

A more intimate factor motivating our move was
that John and I had been drifting apart. Short sentences
requiring only a few words in reply became the norm at
home. "How was your day?" I would ask.

"Okay," he'd grumble while opening the freezer
door and plunging a hand into the ice container.
Pushing the door closed with his shoulder would elicit a
pop as he clanked cubes into a glass and poured
Scotland's finest an eighth of an inch from the top of
the clear rim, turning ice into liquid gold stress relief.
Glass in hand, he'd plant himself in front of the
television—as if he'd missed his rooting spot while at
work—and zone out for the evening. Hours later I
would shake a limp shoulder, startling him, and say,
"John, It's time to go to bed."

Our more lengthy conversations centered on the
kids and their schedules, but the lazy, intimate sharing
of our earlier years—both the significant and minute
details—was gone, having disappeared somewhere into
the term "marriage," where neither of us could
resummons it. Our physical closeness changed too.
John's job was sedentary and he'd stopped exercising,
become doughy. I became distant, avoiding sex and his
touch. We still kissed good night and exchanged a hug
or an encouraging pat, but our bedroom door remained
open most nights. Burning the candle at both ends
ensured the spark would not reignite. *Why had we been
keeping so busy?* Which came first, the chicken or the egg?

Walking miles and miles in the rural Oklahoma
countryside I talked out loud to the Great Spirit (God,
the Universe, whatever you call your higher power),
questioning what I wanted in life. Marriage was sacred

and I'd said my vows with conviction in 1975. Divorce wasn't in my vocabulary. So what were we going to do? No question I'd married John at the right time in my life. He stood for stability and that had been important to me. I had needed an anchor in order to fly my life kite without fluttering completely out of the stratosphere.

Now looking on the practical side, if we were ever to divorce, I sure as hell didn't want to be stuck out in the middle of nowhere without family or a support system.

So we both agreed to work harder on our marriage, to value the positive in our relationship. We entered into counseling and took an Attitude Adjustment course. Perhaps a change of scenery would help both of us.

Once we settled into our new home in Maine and hoping to rekindle the fire, John and I worked in earnest on our relationship by continuing counseling and scheduling date nights. Purposefully we did things together: remodeling the house, spending time in the garden and yard, and attending the kids' sports and school activities. We agreed I should be home with the kids during this time, so I put in an application for a school nurse position in the local district and signed up to be a substitute teacher, either of which would make it possible for me to meet their needs.

Winters in Maine are long, cold, and snowy. John had skied in high school and college and was eager to share this sport with us. While John V and Laura were in school I took ski lessons at a local mountain twice a week and we enrolled the kids in ski school on the weekends, skiing as a family when class was done. The kids took to it readily and so did I. Skiing seemed to help our marriage by providing a common physical exercise and a spiritual connection to nature.

I didn't get the school nurse job but I did get called to substitute fairly regularly. Life between John and me became somewhat steady again—and my thoughts turned to my genealogy project once more.

CAROL LILLIEQVIST WELSH

May 1989

I'd put the quest for my identity on hold after
Margaret's caustic letter but curiosity resurfaced now. I
believed my birth parents were deceased, but some tiny
part of me now doubted that was the truth. Perhaps my
Dream Woman coming to me from a place in the clouds
led me to question it.

Maybe this doubt contributed to making my search
so slow, so methodical. If I'd been searching for parents
who weren't dead, how difficult would it be to tell them
of my abusive childhood? I believed they'd loved me,
wished the best for me. How painful would it be for
them to find out otherwise? *How painful would it be if this
were the case with my own son?* Abuse wouldn't be an easy
thing to lie about should I wish to soften the truth.

My search was for answers, to know my identity and
my ancestry. People do genealogy searches all the time
but usually they already know who they are. I was not a
true McCallum—God knows I wasn't. But who, then,
was I?

Another letter to the adoption agency brought a
prompt reply. This time they threw in a teaser—hinting
that should I come to New York City and meet with
them in person, they might be able to share more
information.

The night before my appointment, I stayed in
Connecticut with my childhood friend Nan. We'd kept
in touch regularly except for a few years when we were
each in our own "hippie" transition, and saw quite a bit
of each other during my summers in Maine. When Nan
and I got together it was like we were little girls,
building sandcastles on the Cape all over again. Time
made no difference in our relationship.

As the train approached the city, my pulse quickened
and I consciously forced myself to breathe deeply in
order to keep nausea at bay.

180

Exiting the dank, dimly lit train tunnel into the rotunda of Grand Central Station, my nose wrinkled at the smell of urine and exhaust that permeated the air. After living for so long in Oklahoma, I'd forgotten how a city smelled.

I might as well have been on the back of a snail for as fast as the bus made its way up Madison Avenue while a flock of frenzied swallows flitted in my gut, as if anxious to be released for their annual sojourn to Capistrano.

A caseworker dressed in a stylish cream and brown pantsuit with shoulder-length graying brown hair, who I will call Paula, greeted me. Her face displayed a sternness that straightened her lips into a thin line, perhaps a telltale sign of years of dealing with emotionally fragile people. At the same time, a warm, compassionate, and reassuring sparkle danced in her eyes. She ushered me into a room of blue stuffed chairs facing a large wooden table. The room was bright as several large windows overlooked a courtyard. From this third floor vantage point, I could only glimpse the top of the trees, their buds unfolding into light green newborn leaves.

Paula surprised me by taking a seat next to rather than opposite me. The stern thin line insisted on discussing my childhood and life with the McCallums at length, while I picked at my fingernails below the table. *This wasn't what I had come for!*

Finally, having had enough of her questions I said, "I don't mind answering your questions, but the letter I received indicated you would give me further information on my birth family if I came all this way. That's why I'm here today—not to talk about the McCallums. Glenn told me my birth parents had been killed in an auto accident, but none of your letters made mention of that. Please, tell me is that true?"

Paula's thin line dropped open, becoming a gaping hole, her eyes widened and the warmth changed to a fiery incredulous stare. Blinking to gain composure, reassurance returned and the hole softened into a less stern line that turned upward, crinkling at the ends, as she smiled and then affirmed my birth mother had been very much alive—she found no record of her having been killed—although the agency would have no way of knowing what might have happened to her after they discontinued contact at around six months after my birth. *I knew it!*

Paula explained that it was common for adoptees to fantasize or aggrandize reasons why their birth parents relinquished them and, reaching out, she patted my hands that were now on the table. *Had I fantasized that?*

"What more can you tell me about them?"

Paula leafed through her papers, reiterating much of what they'd mailed to me five years earlier. "According to the records, your mother was a Midwesterner and was twenty-two when she had you."

Then new information came out. "She told us your father was an undertaker and a pilot during the war."

*Odd, yet interesting.*

"Your mother bragged of her parents' standing in their community telling us her father was a 'master farmer' who'd won many awards."

"What kind of awards?" *Prettiest pig at the county fair?*

"I'm not sure," she said. "It does say here your mother professed to be of Swiss, Scandinavian, and German descent."

"I already know that, but can you tell me what she looked like? Is there a photo of her in your records?"

Sitting silently, my fingers crossed and listening to the crinkling of paper as she shuffled, I imagined a dirty-blonde woman who looked just like me, only older. But then I realized that wouldn't be right, she would have been younger than I in any photograph they would have.

Paula interrupted my imaginings by saying, "It says here that your mother was extremely attractive and animated with a lot of appeal, but I don't have a photo." *Appeal to whom? My adoptive parents? Men? The caseworker? Come on, give me something to hang my hat on—not just bullshit.* "What color hair and eyes did she have? How tall was she? Was she petite like me or big?" My frustration grew.

"I don't believe I have her height and weight, but she had brown hair and brown eyes. That's all it says here. She told the agency worker at the time that she'd received help from an aunt and uncle who gave her money to come to New York so she could avoid telling her parents of her situation. Hmm. It says your mother never told your father about you. She'd discovered he was married and had broken off the relationship before she knew she was pregnant."

I doubted that Paula—who struck me as a good honest person—was making things up or avoiding anything she was able to disclose, but this trip was feeling more and more like a waste of time. All this was stuff they could have put in another letter.

Judging by my own relinquishment experience, my mother might not have been telling the whole truth about her origins or the area she came from, but the agency's description of her was surely accurate. However, judging by the number of papers Paula had shuffled through, certainly she knew a lot more than she was willing to disclose.

Paula rose, extended her hand, and said, "I'm sorry I can't give you more. Should you want to pursue this further I hope you will join the adoption registry. That is the best avenue at this time." Instantly the interview was over.

Walking though Central Park, I again visualized my birthmother incorporating this new information, and stirrings of closeness began to grow deep inside of me. I wondered if she had liked New York or had it been

CAROL LILLIEQVIST WELSH

scary and overwhelming? Could my sense of adventure
and spontaneity have come from her? I guessed she'd
felt excitement here too, even though her burden was
heavy—a far different situation from the one I was in
that spring day.

And Glenn McCallum? No longer did his memory
haunt me. It just was what it was—the memory of a
loving man who became twisted by his inability to
understand his teenage daughter and had acted
irrationally.

In my wanderings I found the jewelry store he'd
once worked for. Curiosity drew me in. To my surprise
the current owner turned out to be the son of one of
Glenn's partners, someone I'd met years ago. We
reminisced about how magical the intricate wrought-iron
gate, uniformed doorman, and dazzling jewelry were to
us as children.

He told me his father was enjoying retirement and
his grandchildren. More importantly he revealed that in
1958, Glenn and another colleague remained junior
partners in the firm, while his father was elevated to
senior partner, eventually becoming the sole owner. This
was something I hadn't known before.

Did what went on between him and me at home
have anything to do with Glenn's less successful climb
up the partnership ladder—an unequal partner to his
friend—and the stresses that would have gone along
with all that? Had the pressures of the job—coupled
with a thirteen-year-old's rebellion and limits testing
before he'd even taken off his overcoat—just been too
much for him?

He must have died a lonely man, though he wouldn't
have acknowledged that. Whatever the cause, I suddenly
felt cheated for what we'd missed, what we might have
had. As I walked away from the jewelry store, a heavy
emptiness hung around my heart.

By the time the train reached Connecticut, I'd
accepted the hurt and let it go once more.

184

Exhausted but unable to sleep that night, I tried again to visualize my birthmother—a pretty, petite woman with straight medium-brown hair and facial features similar to mine. I saw her gazing at me, love radiating as she wrapped her arms around me and pulled me into her at that very moment. A wonderful figment of my imagination.

After returning to Maine, the baby I'd given up and my sister Ginny came into my thoughts once more. Ruminating on the past, I contacted the State of Connecticut, obtaining information on their adoption registry. I then signed a form giving permission for my son to contact me should he ever search, and also provided the new information I had just learned about our shared ancestry. I reached out to Ginny too, tracking her down in Florida.

No great and grand scheme, no specific agenda. Perhaps we could reconnect as sisters, become closer, even if we couldn't regain what we'd had as young children.

"Hi, Ginny? This is Carol, your long lost sister. Sorry to surprise you."

"Oh, hi there," was followed by silence. Then, "Where are you?"

"I'm in Maine." Hearing a sigh (perhaps of relief,) I continued, "You've been on my mind lately. I thought I'd take a chance, see if we could catch up on each other's lives."

We talked for almost an hour ending the conversation with a promise. I'd fly to Florida the following month.

How pleasantly shocking. I mean, she'd blown off my wedding invitation in the '70s, and now after nearly twenty years she wanted to see me. But it might have to do with the fact that both Glenn and Margaret were dead.

As the plane landed, I wondered if I would recognize her. I needn't have worried because she hadn't

185

changed a bit. Still petite and slim, with long blonde hair, I spotted her right away as she waved. We hugged tentatively, neither of us sure how to be with each other after so long. On the ride to her house from the airport, Ginny talked constantly. She'd divorced years ago, remarried, and now owned a local diner-style restaurant where we stopped on the way home to meet her husband.

Her house was airy and light, the typical Southern stucco ranch with a Florida room that faced the golf course. Their furniture was a mixture of old and comfortable new. Sitting on bar stools at an island countertop in the kitchen, we talked of trivial things while Ginny filled the air with clouds of lung-constricting smoke.

Her husband had appeared nervous when we'd first met at the restaurant, but soon relaxed into this strange situation, even proudly sharing his experience of adopting Sandy. Inevitably the conversation turned to Margaret and Glenn, and what life was like for Ginny once I was out of the picture. She hadn't had it as hard as me, but it wasn't any picnic either.

Over three days, we opened up to each other, finding a common ground as mothers. As Ginny expressed herself, I found it strangely uncanny how similar to Glenn and Margaret she had become in some of her attitudes and prejudices, giving me a feeling of déjà vu.

As she drove along Highway 75 on our last day, I said, "You know, Ginny, we've spent three times as many years apart as we have together. I hope this is the end of that."

But it was the end. After this visit we kept in touch for a few years by sending cards at Christmas. Eventually, even those small gestures ceased with both of us going our own way again—not committed by blood or a sisterly bond. This didn't make either of us a bad person. It simply was what it was.

Now trusting in the New York Adoption Registry process to obtain any further information, I spent the next four years or so seeking contentment within myself, growing into a new spirituality. The lack of support in my unhappy preteen and teen years had caused me to turn my back on the church and traditional Judeo-Christian ideas about God and religion. Where was God when Glenn was beating and spurning me? I hadn't become an atheist in the purest sense but had definitely put religion on a back burner.

While studying for my master's degree, I'd explored many different religious philosophies, including Native American culture. Perhaps because of my experiences living in nature at the Maine cabin, or my years spent in Oklahoma in close proximity to Native peoples, I came to respect and identify with their belief system more than any other and incorporated several of those beliefs into my own life. Upon moving to Maine, I serendipitously met a woman who asked me to become part of a spiritual group that shared this respect for Native practices.

Continuing with discussions and prayer in my weekly spiritual group, I also participated in self-help experiences, including a week on a mountaintop with a like-minded group of women, and I traveled to Georgia three different times to attend an event called The Rivercane Rendezvous, where I learned the native skills of brain-tanning deer hide, fashioning darts out of reeds and cattail fluff, making a blowgun from river cane, and using a froe to peel long thin slivers of oak from a log then weave them into a beautiful carrying basket.

Through all of these adventures and practices I experienced a paradigm shift: from shame and insecurity to pride and gratitude. Now I walked my own true path. But where would it take me?

CAROL LILLIEQVIST WELSH

## The Big D

Summer 1992 – Dixfield, Maine

Walking my own true path included my picture-perfect family—except I was falling out of love with my husband. Even though we continued with counseling, making progress in some areas, he wasn't constantly on my mind anymore, nor did I light up at the sight of him when he came through the door at the end of the day.

Our life together had become practical. All physical attraction to him was gone. I even rebuked his touch. Instead of making love I'd lie awake at night, feigning sleep, questioning, digging for solutions, ways to change things and make my marriage work. Some nights I felt like a dog with a big pile of sand behind her and no bone in the hole. Marriage was supposed to be forever! This wasn't just a mid-life crisis. We both deserved more in a relationship.

Determined not to act impulsively, I went out into nature again calling on my Dream Woman. Hiking in the summer sun up a green and rocky ski trail on nearby Mt. Abram, I reached the summit and leaned against a warm rock, focusing my attention on the glacially sculpted, bouldered peaks of distant Mt. Washington. My skin hot from the climb, I welcomed the cooling, sweat-drying breeze.

*I open my heart to power of the Universe, to the four directions, to father sun and grandmother moon, and to you Dream Woman. Please send me guidance and direction.*

Years of marriage floated past closed eyelids. Patiently I waited until my aching butt forced me to move off the rock. No sign had miraculously come.

188

Halfway down the mountain, I encountered an outcropping of rocks with a small cliff probably fifteen feet above the grassy ground below. On impulse, I backed up and ran toward the edge, jumping off the cliff while spreading my arms like a bird. Airborne for only a few seconds, I felt as if I were being lifted up, carried by someone or something as time stood still, and then landed gently on the ground in a semi-crouched position, totally unhurt and nearly twenty feet from the cliff. *Was this my sign?* I stood and gazed back at the rocky landscape before snaking my way down the mountain, feeling like I had shed an old skin, leaving it to dry and disintegrate.

The following morning I made a date with John for dinner that Friday night. He chose a restaurant in Farmington we'd wanted to try. I might as well have been a headless chicken—my intensifying anxiety made me unable to concentrate on anything all week.

A grand rehearsal spun in my head as I struggled to place an order with the waiter. In the pregnant silence that had become common between us, we both nursed our iced teas.

Unable to postpone the inevitable any longer, I placed my hand on his and carefully choosing the right words, my voice just above a whisper, I said, "John, it's obvious you're as unhappy with our marriage as I am. Lord knows we've tried everything to make it work, counseling, workshops, even moving. I love you. I always will, but we just can't live like this any more. You need intimacy just as much as I do." Mascara streaked my cheeks. "I don't know what else to do. I'm sorry! I'm afraid it's time for a divorce."

A grapefruit sized lump in my throat, I sincerely wished for John to say divorce wasn't necessary, that he would make everything all right again, that he would take me in his arms, ease the sadness of the last several years, and ignite a new fire. Holding my breath, I sat suspended in time and space.

189

CAROL LILLIEQVIST WELSH

His big hazel eyes glazed over as they filled with tears and half closed. Nodding slowly, sandwiching my hand with his, his whole body shook. I wanted to crawl into a hole.

My wish wouldn't be granted. We considered going to a different counselor and even having a trial separation, but both of us recognized that probably neither solution would change things. Instead, we sobbed our way home.

Over the next few weeks, our disappointments brought out hidden strengths as we made rational and reasonable plans. Both of us were concerned about the kids, as they were still only fifteen and eight, we felt it important to ensure an amicable "unmarriage."

One thing we didn't anticipate was how difficult it would be to tell them we were separating. We knew it would be hard, just not *that* hard.

Calling them into the living room on a Saturday afternoon, John and I sat opposite each other with Laura next to me, JV next to him. As gently as possible, I started, "Dad and I have something we need to talk to you about."

My heart pounded, swooshing in my ears as I continued, "You know that Daddy and Mommy have been going to counseling for a while now and after lots of talking, we haven't been able to fix our problems. We have decided to live in separate houses." *Please don't let my children feel betrayed!*

John V licked his middle finger then rubbed his nose with it (his typical nervous habit) and said, "Why? Are you getting divorced?" Was it *that* obvious?

John swallowed hard, "We don't know that, Johnny. But we aren't happy living together right now."

"So you *are* getting divorced!" he said.

Reaching out, he placed his hand over John V's and said, "We're going to separate. Mom and I are going to live in different houses for a while. We'll take turns

190

being here in your house with you and see how that goes. But in the end, yes, we may get a divorce."

Although trying to maintain a calm façade, I was falling apart inside yet I said emphatically, "It's important for both of you to understand you haven't done anything wrong. This is not your fault."

The rest of the evening passed in a blur, with John and I falsely portraying reassurance and strength while internally feeling like yellow Jell-O.

Pensively, John V went to his room, taking a few family photo albums with him. Laura curled up on the sofa between us, sniffling, until she fell asleep and John carried her to bed.

Out of our concern for the kids and their reactions to the news, John and I promised we would never put each other down or talk about one another behind the other's back. We'd present a united front, not give mixed messages or create additional issues for the kids to deal with.

We frequently provided opportunities for them to express their emotions and explore the situation. I was especially sensitive about Laura having feelings of rejection or abandonment. Of course I worried about John V too, but he was older and better able to express himself. Plus, he didn't have first-hand experience with the issue of abandonment that Laura did through adoption.

John rented a house in town close to his work, while I housesat for a friend who was selling her home in a neighboring town.

Although we knew of no model for it, we'd worked this all out ourselves. The kids liked their home, their neighborhood, their friends and their school. Why should we uproot them from all that? We'd seen kids with two of everything—two sets of friends, two bicycles in two different garages. And in those cases, more was less.

So Laura and JV stayed put, their physical lives remaining somewhat unchanged as we strived for as little short-or long-term impact on them as possible. We didn't want our kids to experience divorce quite like other children. Nastiness and arguments at home, custody battles in court? In this case, our kids had *custody* of us!

Had John never been in my life I wouldn't have evolved. Only with him as my anchor was I able to explore my inner self. I am forever grateful to him for those chapters of my life and look back on our marriage with many happy memories—and only a few regrets. Would I have wanted it to last forever? Of course! Do I wish I'd done a better job at being a wife? Of course! Would I have done it differently? Well, maybe some things. But the outcome would probably have been the same.

Wyoming

July 1993

With John V and Laura adjusting well to the divorce and John's willingness to cover my schedule with them, I seized the opportunity for adventure.

A road trip would take me across the northern part of the country to include a few days in the Badlands of North Dakota before meeting up with a friend in Wyoming for backpacking "real" mountains. Not having seen each other since the Rivercane Rendezvous in Georgia years earlier, time flew by for Stacy and me as we caught up on each other's lives.

Just west of Sheridan, the Big Horn Mountains rise sharply, showing off geological layers of multicolored earth beneath verdant pines and grasses. Stacy chose this mountain range for our adventure because grizzly bears don't live in the Big Horns. She had backpacked all over the world and this was a wonderful opportunity for her to give me hands-on lessons in survival and being alone in the wilderness. I learned a lot that week.

Waving goodbye as Stacy's plane took off for Virginia, my pulse quickened with excitement. Almost blinded by the setting sun I drove west, back into the Big Horn Mountains. Diverting off of the main highway, I followed a set of dirt ruts leading into an uninhabited valley miles from nowhere. Ablaze with wildflowers and lush green grasses contrasting the dark green conifers, I'd found the perfect place for a good night's sleep under twinkling stars. Now the real test began—on my own in this wild country.

I woke to a chorus of crickets harmonizing with twittering songbirds. Heat from the mid-morning sun had created a greenhouse effect in the small tent and I was soaked with sweat. I'd brought a unique exerciser with me called "The Flo" and, with Dan Folgeberg serenading me through my new fangled earbuds, I danced into full wakefulness—a strange looking creature in a pristine setting.

By the end of that week, I'd soaked in healing hot springs, viewed ancient petroglyphs, and spent quiet meditative time at an ancient Native American Medicine Wheel high on a plateau. This incredible solitary time offered every opportunity to challenge myself physically, emotionally, and spiritually. My confidence soared with each new step into the wilderness.

One morning I crossed the Great Divide, then wound along an anxiety-producing switch-back road to a ranger kiosk in the Wind River Range State Park.

"Welcome. How long will you be staying?" the smiling forest ranger asked.

"Two nights at least, maybe more," I replied.

A sapphire sky touched the jagged, dark grey, marshmallow-topped peaks of the mountains above thick verdant forests. Meadows burst forth with late summer colors sliced into pie-like wedges by silver streams cascading though them. Inhaling a deep rib-expanding breath of crisp, pollution-free air, I gathered my gear and again hiked high into the clouds.

No longer was I the crazy kid who drove cross-country dancing in clubs, the twenty-something who'd pick up on a lark, moving where the wind blew her.

Still embracing adventure, I also searched for inner knowledge, spiritual growth, and more of the calm self-confident woman I'd just sampled.

## Log Home

Now I knew what I wanted in life: a good relationship with my children and a home of our own where we could establish new roots. It would have to have privacy, woods, and water—replicating the serenity of the cabin in Boothbay. Ski instructing didn't pay very well and was only seasonal, subbing was sporadic at best, and there weren't any nursing jobs available within a reasonable commute, so the spring after John and I divorced, I started a lawn-care business. Thirty-five lawns paid the bills and kept me busy from April through November while still allowing me to be active in John V and Laura's busy lives. It also gave me the flexibility to build our home.

With funds in a retirement account that could be borrowed against, a monetary agreement with John, and if I was frugal, I was confident I could pull this off. Contacting realtors, the search for the perfect property began.

Hundreds of houses were available, but I found nothing that I resonated with, so while continuing to search, many of my nights were occupied with designing a dream home, trusting that the right property would turn up at the right time.

March 1984 - a dream

*As a bird flying high over the land, gazing down on a beautiful meadow, I made lazy circles in the sky before descending to perch on the branch of a tall white pine growing on the edge of*

195

*a cliff crest. Below in a small pond, tiny fish glistened in the
sunlight. Eventually spreading my expansive wings, I soared
toward the sun.*

Upon waking, tranquility filed every pore as I
reflected on this beautiful place of my dream.

Several months later, while driving to the kids'
house for my turn as parent, I took a different route
than usual and noticed a for-sale sign by the side of the
road. It suddenly dawned on me that this was a piece of
land the real estate agent had given me a listing sheet
for, one that I'd declined to look at due to cost. A half-
mile past the road, curiosity turned me around.

As the car crept up the dirt road, a sensation of
déjà vu rose in my gut. The road wound right, then left,
and right again where a rocky cliff face crowned with
tall pines appeared. Rounding the final curve and
passing an old stone wall I turned easterly, coming to
what once had been a dooryard.

Standing on a small knoll, I saw a mass of concrete
rubble—a cellar hole, charred remains of a house with
glass shards everywhere, a shed surrounded by piles of
lumber, and a homemade swing set. Beyond the
foundation, in the greening meadow, a small pond
reflected puffy clouds and sky.

Despite its condition, an aura of positive energy
flowed in this place. This was where I belonged, where I
was supposed to be. Here I would transform this
burned-out foundation so symbolic of my earlier life,
click the heels of ruby-red slippers, and build my own
Emerald City—a log home in which to raise my children
in harmony with the Universe.

A new flame had ignited and I was energized.
Instead of needing John or someone else to do it, by
building this house, I would now nail *myself* down.

Gathering my graph-paper designs, I voraciously read everything I could about log cabins, researching what materials to use—which would be best for the environment and my pocketbook.

July 1994

Within hours of closing on the property, I started pounding nails, quickly converting the shed near the woods into a living space with a sleeping loft, so Laura and I could live right there.

John and I agreed that before school began, he would move back into the kids' house with John V, while Laura would change school districts and move in with me. The kids could be together on the weekends at either of our houses or whenever they chose during the week, as long as we could arrange transportation.

With intermittent help from John V, Laura, and friends, work began slowly on the foundation. Debris was scattered all over the property and the intensity of the fire years before had cracked and possibly weakened the concrete foundation walls. They needed to be chiseled, filled, and sealed. A structural engineer recommended adding additional interior timber supports for strength along the major north and south walls. Dirt needed to be pulled away then pushed back after tarring the outside of the foundation.

Frustrated at how slowly things were progressing—considering I'd never built anything more than a few beds and a kitchen counter—and anxious to see my dream become a reality, I hired a wild and crazy out-of-work ski instructor colleague. He had a modicum of building experience and was up to the full-time challenge of helping me. I also hired a neighboring high school student on evenings and weekends. Finally, the project moved right along.

With every swing of the sledgehammer my new roots spread into the earth, truly grounding me.

CAROL LILLIEQVIST WELSH

It took four months working every day, in all kinds of weather, until on my forty-ninth birthday I stood back, amazed at my accomplishment. Pride swelled, giving purpose to my aching muscles.

The next day, those muscles ached anew as we moved from the shed into our piney-smelling new log home.

I wasn't prepared for the let down when there were no longer any nails to pound. I'd lost direction and didn't know which way to turn—what to tackle first. Nor was I prepared for what happened when we turned on the heat. The uncured logs wept. As resinous water seeped in rivulets, staining the beautiful, symmetric, lovingly constructed walls, tears of disappointment angrily rolled out of my eyes.

The next few weeks brought a modicum of relief as a cleaning crew bleached the logs while I followed with brush strokes of polyurethane, forcing any remaining liquid to weep on the outside.

With eighty-seven acres to play on, the time seemed right for Laura to have her long wished-for dog. The chocolate lab-beagle mix we rescued and named Hershey took a liking to Laura right off—they even shared the same auburn-colored hair. I hadn't had canine companionship since Little Bit. A familiar love and companionship soon developed between Hershey and me.

I'd not only nailed myself down, squaring with history again, but I'd nailed down my daughter as well.

## Skiing and Searching

The search for my biological roots had become more passive and cerebral, more intuitive, over the previous several years.

Weekly spiritual group meetings became my therapist. Friends didn't parrot back what I said (as therapists had), didn't preach or judge, but trusted in the power of something greater than us, and in the process rather than the possible end results of whatever paths we were following. We practiced gratitude for what we have, asking for what we needed, then letting go and trusting we would receive whatever was best for all. Who knew that in 2006, Rhonda Byrne would put this understanding into a book (and movie) called *The Secret* and sell millions of copies?

By finding out about my biological history, I would hopefully come to a clearer insight of my true self.

John V provided the opportunity to parent a child. Laura's adoption provided an opportunity to re-parent my own adopted self. Both children are gifts who allowed me to grow alongside them, but Laura and I were uniquely connected. Cosmic strings were pulled when she came into my life.

I'd never completely dealt with the shame I carried from the past and I began to open up about giving up a child to more and more people, bringing issues out of the closet, so to speak. Not that I painted billboards, but in talking about these issues out loud with people I trusted, the issues themselves became clearer to me.

Dick was one of those trusted people.

Our relationship began as activity buddies at Mt. Abram, where we met in 1990 while working for the ski school. While John and the kids skied together, Dick and I improved our own abilities and learned effective ways of teaching others. Over those winters we became fast friends, sharing thoughts and concerns, and helping each other strive for higher professional status in our work. Dick was easy to talk to and soon became someone I could bounce things off of while going through the maze of divorce.

After building my house and recognizing the small shed-cabin as a source of income, I began renting it. After two years, my tenant gave his notice. Dick had been living in an over-priced trailer after separating from his wife and seeing an opportunity to pay forward the support he'd shown me during my divorce, I offered to rent him the cabin.

With Dick living right next door and his divorce final later that year, we began seeing each other in a different light. No longer just a good friend, I noticed that he was tall, dark, handsome, and physically sculpted to perfection. Spiritually connected, he saw beauty in the environment and derived enjoyment from digging in the dirt. Accomplished at running heavy equipment he could do just about anything with his hands...well, that too. He had the cutest scar on the right side of his cheek from a childhood sledding accident, but it was his Steve McQueen turquoise eyes that melted me. We found ourselves spending all our free time dreamily gazing into each other's eyes, holding hands, acting like new lovers do.

The kids knew and liked Dick, so were readily accepting of the relationship. In winter, we all skied as a family—even including John many times. John V also caught the instructing bug and at fifteen, began teaching skiing—and later snowboarding—for a free pass and pocket money.

Outgrowing our local ski mountain, the three of us changed jobs and worked at nearby Sunday River, a larger resort. I'd concentrated on professionalizing my passion by coming up through the ranks, successfully securing my Level One and Level Two PSIA (Professional Ski Instructors Association) certifications alongside Dick. While we were there, Sunday River expanded by leaps and bounds and naturally experienced growing pains. Within a few years, instead of teaching quality skiing, Dick and I were asked to promote equipment sales and timeshare ownerships during our lessons. By 1996 the enjoyment had gone out of teaching the sport.

"What do you think of going out West to teach next winter?" I asked Dick, while thumbing through a ski magazine. "I'm sick of selling timeshares instead of giving a good ski lesson. It's sleazy having a hidden agenda every time we teach. You know, we had so much fun skiing powder on that vacation we took to Utah. I'd love to do that for a whole season."

"I know. I hate the timeshare thing. Where are you suggesting we go?"

"There are lots of ads in this ski magazine for Colorado. We know a few people who've worked out West. What about Rob? He'd give us a good recommendation and could suggest where we should apply. Worst-case scenario we don't find a job and stay here. What do you think?"

"Okay, I'm in. Let's talk to him."

This of course impacted our kids. Dick's two children were older, one in college, one working, and would certainly want to visit for a ski vacation, but what about Laura and John V? They were both excited about the adventure.

Discussing our plans with John, it was decided that, given Laura's struggles with academics and friends over the last year, she and Hershey would live with Dick and me, while JV (who was nearing the end of high school) would stay with his dad. He'd spend vacations out West with us, riding the powder and, of course, giving his sister a brotherly hard time about everything.

With stellar letters of recommendation from our friend Rob, Keystone Resort in Dillon hired us—sight unseen—after only two telephone interviews.

Middle school in Colorado turned out to be beneficial for Laura, as did skiing steeper, gnarlier terrain. Both things built her confidence. Instructing in Colorado turned out to be good for Dick's and my professional progress. Everyone's disposition improved too under skies that were either bright blue with crisp sunshine or dropping light velvety snow. No more rain and fog to ski in.

Captured by the friendliness of people we met and worked with, and particularly given Laura's social acceptance and academic progress at school, we repeated the scenario the following season. Although attending school in two different states worked well during middle school once she reached high school, it would be another story.

School Administrative District 17's high school in Norway, Maine offered a comprehensive vocational-technical program, something everyone felt would best suit Laura's needs. So dealing with my local bank, I purchased a foreclosure house and offered a yearly lease on our log home to my seasonal tenant. Laura and I moved to Norway with mixed emotions, rationalizing that it was only temporary until Laura finished high school. Dick had purchased a home of his own in Maine after our first winter in Colorado, my converted shed having been only a temporary solution from the beginning. We felt we had the best of both worlds—our own space in the summers, and all of us living together in the winters.

The Norway place was pretty run down and needed a lot of work. But after having built the log house, we were somewhat accomplished in construction, so we rolled up our sleeves, turning the second story into a small one-bedroom rental apartment and the first floor into a comfy home for Laura and me. I hired a helper to share the load of my lawn accounts in the Bethel area and took on a few more in Norway. Laura helped me with the lawn business, earning pocket money as she adjusted to the new house. She soon became excited about starting school and making new friends.

That winter I stayed home with Laura, having negotiated a unique deal with Keystone, and commuted to Colorado in two-week intervals. When I was gone, John and his new wife cared for her.

Ironically, I made more money commuting to Colorado part-time than I could have made full-time at the local mountains in Maine, even taking all the airfare into consideration.

Laura's transition into her teens began with the predictable typical rebellion against any authority, including her father and his new wife Becky, her teachers and classmates, as well as Dick and me. "I hate you," and "You can't make me," were heard often. Laura liked being the center of attention and dramatically kept the pot stirred when she wasn't. Harboring something I'd said, or Becky had done, she allowed resentment to brew it until words and actions erupted like lava from a volcano.

When we sought counseling, Laura's adoption surfaced. "Mom, I want to know more about my birth mother. Do I look like her?" she asked.

"I'm not sure, honey, but Dad saw her and said her hair was auburn like yours."

"Why did she give me up and keep her other children?"

Taking her hand in mine, gently patting it, I said, "She had two other small children. It was just too much for her."

"I hate her. It's all her fault. If she'd kept me I wouldn't have to be with you and I wouldn't have to put up with stupid Becky!"

Putting out the emotional fires of my teenage daughter made me wonder, *was this how I was with my parents?*

Over time, Laura calmed down.

"If you really want to find out more about your birthmother, I'll help you." After all, I'd been the one who'd pushed for an open adoption in the first place.

John on the other hand was against this new venture. He felt that adoption was clouding the waters, a non-issue raised to keep us from focusing on what he saw as really ailing Laura: problems at school, with friends, and the difficulties with him and Becky. John felt Laura's desire to know about her birthmother would pass. And so it did, for a while.

But Laura's troubles with school and peers escalated, plaguing her until finally we stepped in, sending her to summer wilderness camp and then to a private boarding school. It was there, through maturity and the family's involvement with group counseling, that she straightened herself out. Or so it seemed.

1999 – 2000

Following Bread Crumbs

December 1999

During Laura's junior year of boarding school she
again raised the issue of her birthmother. What had once
before been an obfuscation of the real issues she was
facing, felt worth exploring now, even if just to put it to
rest.

So Laura and I set out together to find *both* our
birthmothers, this time with everyone's support.

She experienced a lot of stopping and starting, as
well as frustration. The desire to delve into her heritage
waxed and waned; one day she'd be all pepped up about
it, then the next she couldn't have cared less. Finding
certain pieces of information then hitting dead ends, I
began to suspect her parents might have divorced,
making the search harder.

I understood her frustrations. Many years of
receiving letters that never led to anything specific had
put my search on the back burner too.

About ten years had passed since my last contact
with Spence-Chapin Agency. I reintroduced myself by
phone, asking whether changes in the law might allow
them to disclose more than in 1989. They mailed
updated information on the New York State Adoption
Registry and a questionnaire, which I immediately filled
out and returned.

The following week a written reply came from the
agency, basically reiterating everything they'd told me in
the '80s. This time though, they were a bit more specific
and provided a few colorful and helpful pieces to the
puzzle. My mother was the second of six children, five

girls and a boy. She was a teacher and had a job while in New York awaiting my birth, etc., etc. Having falsified information when I was in the same situation, I viewed all these platitudes with a jaundiced eye. It made for a nice story but who knew what was true? Although this time, my gut believed more than doubted.

At the insistence of John V, a computer whiz, I'd become somewhat Internet savvy. Reading between the lines of the data the agency sent, and hoping for a tangible lead, I plugged some of the information into a few search engines.

Needing more to go on, I called the agency again, attempting to ingratiate myself in hopes of finding a sympathetic ear. Adoption is a people business; if I had been calling a manufacturer to complain about my steel-belted radials, it's doubtful I'd have sought to make any friends, but this was different.

Luck was with me. Speaking to a nice sounding young woman, I schmoozed and negotiated, hopeful that she would be kind enough to do for me what would of course be patently illegal, yet humane. Empathetic and willing to answer anything she could short of crossing that legal line, she agreed to play twenty questions with me.

"Are you into astrology? Can you tell me what sign my mother was born under?" I asked. Obviously it would help to know a date of birth.

"Um, she was a sun sign."

Cancer the Crab. "Cancer's between June 22 and July 22. Can you clarify if she was born early or later in Cancer?" I asked. *She* knew my mother's name, date of birth and address, and other vital statistics—in fact was probably staring right at it. She simply could not tell *me*.

"Very early," she replied.

Um, most likely late in June. Hey, it might not sound like much, but when playing detective every bit helped.

The first letter I'd received had established that my birthmother and her family were from the Midwest. "Did she live in the northern or southern part of the Midwest?

"Southern."

"If I name the correct state would you cough?" A less-patient person on either end of the line would have hung up in disgust but luckily I wasn't going to stand on ceremony and neither was my game-playing opponent.

"Is it Oklahoma?"

"No. But it's right out there," she said.

"Texas, Nebraska, Kansas..."

"Cough, cough, cough."

*Kansas. My birth family was from Kansas.*

Reaching far back into memory for anything else Glenn or Margaret might have told me about my adoption, I recalled hearing the last name of my birth parents was Johnson. I asked if this were true.

"Yes. That is listed as one of the names your birthmother used, but your mother and father were not married to each other at the time of your birth."

Okay, this presented a quandary. Johnson was as common as Jones. It might have been my mother's maiden name, or an easy name to come up with, or the last name of my birthfather. But it was something.

"I don't suppose you can tell me the first name of the man listed as my father can you?"

She hesitated then said, "Well, it's a name you're quite familiar with."

You either loved this game or hated it.

"Is it my adopted father's name? Is it Glenn?" That would be way too weird.

"Yes and no."

Geez! Was this guy a cross-dresser named Glenda? But wait..."So it's not Glenn I take it."

"No."

Hmm...Glenn was actually my adoptive father's middle name, which he'd used as his first.

"Would William be the name we're looking for?"

She hesitated, and then coughed quietly.

William Johnson. Was my biological father's name William, maybe Bill, Johnson? Both such damn common names. Were they just the quickest thing my birthmother could come up with under pressure? Did she know someone by that name? Ugh!

We covered a lot of ground concerning my mother's father's mother (my would-be great-grandmother) who allegedly had earned a living as a great Impressionist artist. Again, this could have been just so much bunk, but even as a skeptic, I had to admit that such a tale would have taken a lot more effort to fabricate than simply saying you were "with child" by a guy named William Johnson, which was just one step removed from John Doe. My grandmother was said to have been a native of Switzerland. Now, I didn't claim to know a lot about art but surely the world didn't host a gaggle of famous female Swiss Impressionists.

*Something to follow up on!*

Asking next about my mother's father, I learned he'd graduated from a Swiss agricultural college, had been fifty-four when I was born, was active in 4-H and had won honors and awards for farming. *So he'd have been born in 1891, and how many Swiss agricultural colleges could there be?* Now we were getting somewhere.

"What kind of awards did he win?"

"It says here it was the Skelly Award for Achievement in Agriculture."

*I knew years ago Paula was holding back. Thank goodness this woman wasn't.* God knew how tough the competition might have been, but still an award was an award and it bore a name, so some sort of paper trail indicating who had given it out and who received it must exist somewhere.

The woman told me my mother had been proud to speak about this award because he had won it not long before she moved to New York.

Bells went off in my head. Now I knew the name of an award and approximately the year it was given to my grandfather. "Okay, so I've got some leads to follow up on. You'll probably hear from me again," I said, then thanked her for playing my game.

Between packing for Colorado and meeting the needs of my family, I ran out of time and had to curb my eagerness to continue searching.

Arriving at our Colorado condo with time on my hands, I Googled the W.G. Skelly Award. This provided some information but not enough. Next, Googling Swiss Impressionist artists, I happened on a site that referenced a book titled *An International Dictionary of Women Artists Born Before 1900.*

Denver Library owned the book and it was in my mailbox the next day.

Racing through it, I discovered a short entry for the artist Adelé Lilljeqvist (maiden name Wieland) who was born in Berne, Switzerland in 1862 and died there in 1927. She painted landscapes and still lifes, was a former president of the Society of Swiss Women Painters and Sculptors and the *only* Swiss Impressionist artist listed. John's sister, Sue, was a curator of prints and drawings at the Museum of Fine Arts in Boston. Perhaps she'd be able to help.

Opening an email to contact her, I noticed something in the inbox from one of the people I'd queried about the Skelly Award. In 1944, the W.G. Skelly Award for Achievement in Agriculture was given to a Walter Lillieqvist. Wow! Close enough for a cigar.

With a quickly Googled "Kansas family histories-Lillieqvist," up popped a genealogy site and a link directing me to a book titled *The Chosen Land,* an anthology of stories written by Barber County, Kansas residents. A Matilda Lillieqvist wrote one of the chapters. Little hairs on the back of my neck stood on end, my stomach flip-flopped. The chapter titled "Walter Lillieqvist," described farm life in Kansas and spoke of his trip back to his native Switzerland to visit an ailing mother in 1927. My heart raced with excitement.

I rang up Spence-Chapin hoping to catch my contact and confront her with a simple question—one she'd been reticent to answer right from the start. But now I was no longer asking, "What was my mommy's name?" This time the question was, "Is my mother's last name Lillieqvist?"

Luck was with me she hadn't left for the day. She responded, "I'd like to tell you, Carol. But you know I can't give you that information."

For as helpful as she'd been up to that point I'd finally had it with the game playing. I just needed confirmation of a name, one specific name. "C'mon. We've played around and around and we've come this far. You're staring right at the answer and if I were there in your office, I'd be tempted to yank the file out of your hand and run with it, so let's spare us both a foot race and come to some understanding."

We were at an impasse. This was the one step beyond which she felt she could not legally go. I was equally flummoxed.

Taking a deep breath and softening my voice, I said, "Okay. If you hang up on me right now without saying goodbye, I'll take it that I have the right last name. So please, either talk to me or hang up." The phone went dead followed by a dial tone.

Winter Storm

I called Dick right away.

While he was driving toward Colorado, I surfed different websites and found the dates of Walter and Matilda's deaths. She had died in 1997, only three years earlier. That tight feeling I get in my throat just before tears fall, caused me to pause for a short time. If only I'd had this information earlier I might have known her.

Even though Matilda had died in Pratt, Kansas, no matter where I searched I couldn't come up with an obituary. But an actual town was far better than just a county—it was time to investigate in person.

10 December 2000 – Colorado to Kansas

We left Dillon at 11:30 in the morning, hoping to get ahead of a major winter storm. As the car climbed the steep grade on I-70 approaching the Eisenhower Tunnel, sun streamed from the west through the windshield, leading Dick and me to believe the weather forecasters were wrong again. But the Rockies hold many surprises. As we exited the eastern end of the tunnel descending toward Denver, clouds boiled ahead of us while the temperature dropped rapidly. Fog turned to ice giving the appearance of a lead-in to a rock concert—ethereal and otherworldly, challenging our reality—fitting since what we were about to do was surreal as well.

I jiggled my leg, feeling excitement interspersed with doubts and fear, as different scenarios played in my head. What if my mother were actually living in Pratt? How should I contact her? I doubted my birth and adoption were public knowledge in a small town. Discretion would definitely be the best part of valor. I could pretend to be a writer researching Kansas's farm life. That wouldn't be a lie. For years I'd been journaling, and at the urging of friends had been considering writing a book about my life.

Was Matilda the woman who came to me in dreams, my guide and comforter? Having lived on the plains of Kansas during the Dust Bowl days of the Depression, she had to have been a strong and determined woman. According to my research, Walter had received his agricultural award for terrace-style farming, which made his land more bountiful.

Reading what Matilda wrote in *The Chosen Land,* I found it easy to envision a farmer's wife taking care of her children alone while Walter went back to Switzerland to care for his mother during the last few months of her life.

Maybe it was my great-grandmother in the dream. She, too, must have been a strong woman to raise children and become a famous artist, given the times.

But I'd secretly wished—no hoped—that it was my own mother in the dream. The woman we might soon find.

The next day in Russell, Kansas, I woke early, rolled over, and snuggled up next to Dick as he wrapped his arms around me, pulling me into him, warm skin next to warm skin.

He asked, "Are you nervous about today?"

"Yeah, excited to know more and hopefully find my mother. But part of me is petrified of the unknown. I'm really working hard at letting go of the outcome, trusting that what's meant to be will be and bracing for disappointment. My worst fear is that she won't want to see me. That would be the ultimate rejection."

Lifting my chin with his finger, a mischievous twinkle in his eyes, he kissed me. In that one kiss an incredible unconditional love passed between us, and I knew everything would be all right. My mind drifted away to a white sandy beach where I gazed into his turquoise eyes, the color of travel posters of faraway places. As we made love, cluttered thoughts disappeared. On the road again, we drove in silence through ebony darkness. As the sky lightened, endless miles of farmland lay covered in bluish-white snow, reflecting the refracted light of a clear sky. Corn stubble poked through the expansive cold blanket, giving the landscape an unshaven morning shadow. With their tired seed heads bent over, heavy with frost, dormant sunflower plants glistened as the sun crested the horizon.

We drove past farmhouses with lights flicking on as the people started their day. Occasionally, the odd car would pass going in the opposite direction, but mostly the road belonged to us.

Approaching Pratt, the landscape sprouted dinosaur-shaped pumps rhythmically sucking black gold or gas out of the earth. Cattle grazed on hay near lonely windmills, tumbleweeds shook off the storm's snow as they rolled and skipped in the wind toward the light of day. An oil refinery loomed on a far knoll, an elderly Air Force plane sat in solitude marking the entrance to an industrial airport. As we crested a small hill, a grain elevator and water tower broke the blue background signifying Pratt.

The closer we got the more my stomach knotted.

Dick read my mind. Pulling into a mom-and-pop quick-stop on the edge of town for a cup of coffee, he said, "You've been awfully quiet. Are you okay?"

"Yeah, just nervous as hell. You know, having been genetically programmed by two people then set adrift to be raised with another family's identity…well, I'm not sure I'll know how to relate to a birthmother. But if there is a strong physical resemblance, it will be easier for me to claim ownership and identify with her."

215

Patting my hand and then pulling me close, he gave me one of his big, warm bear hugs, willing me his strength. Relaxing into his arms, the tension subsided.

A few moments later, tears rolled down my cheeks. I choked out, "Oh, honey, what if she's dead? It would mean I've reached an end without any answers. I don't know if I could handle that after all this build-up these last two weeks."

*She just had to be alive. No! She was alive, and she would want to see me!*

Kissing me softly, wiping away tears, he said, "I love you. I know you can do this."

I nodded. "Okay, let's get you some coffee and something to calm my stomach."

Ada May

11 December 2000 – Barber County, Kansas

The streets of Pratt were paved with brick, not uncommon for this part of the country. Stores already decorated for Christmas greeted us in reds and greens. Lights strung across the main street twinkled.

According to Spence-Chapin, my mother had attended college for a teaching degree but I had no clue which one or where. Logic dictated that I should start with the community college in Pratt. Hopefully their library would hold some kind of records that would add to what I already knew. Certainly it would at least have copies of the local paper and an obituary for Matilda.

I located the obituary in the college library without any problem. There the information I'd been seeking almost jumped off the page.

"That's her! It has to be her! Ada M. Mitchell. Holy shit! We found her!" My heart beat faster. *I knew her name!*

"Oh, honey! There's no turning back now. We've passed failsafe!"

"The obituary is only three years ago," Dick said. "Let's hope your mother is still alive and in good health."

"Oh, my God! It says here that she lives in Medicine Lodge, Kansas."

Looking over my shoulder, Dick said, "So, next stop Medicine Lodge?"

"It says in the obituary a son, Lucky Lillieqvist, lives right here in Pratt. Let's check out his house."

Dick found Lucky's address in the phone book. Lucky was his actual name not a nickname. His was a yellow-brick ranch house typical of that part of the Midwest, located on a corner lot in a nice residential section of town. No one was home so, acting like a sneaky private detective, I stepped out of the truck and snapped a photo before we turned to the highway and headed south.

Medicine Lodge kept running through my head. "Hey, I've been to Medicine Lodge! When we were living in Oklahoma, I went there for a reenactment of the signing of the 1867 Peace Treaty between the Five Tribes of the Plains Indians and the United States Government. It must have been 1985. I'd spent the night camping in a field somewhere near where they held the pageant and also went into town to visit a museum—an old fort or something. The whole thing was pretty interesting. Townsfolk dressed as pioneers, circled covered wagons in a flat area surrounded by red dirt knolls. At one point, Indians rode in on horseback raiding the wagon train. That's about all I remember. If I'd only known Ada M. Mitchell lived there! How weird would that have been?"

"Weirder if she was one of the actors," Dick said.

Why had it taken me so long to find this woman? I was certain she'd given me up in love. What would it feel like to find out the child you gave up in love had been abused? It wasn't something I wished to subject her to, nor experience myself.

But what else was going on inside of me all those years? Fear of rejection of course, but had I been afraid of a relationship with her? Would she have wanted to claim me as hers, expected me to live by her rules, be a daughter to her in a way I couldn't have been? Take care of her in old age? Could I have done any of that? Would her love be unconditional or would she judge me, be ashamed of my actions as a teenager and a young twenty-something woman? All this ran through my head.

Fields gave way to houses as we approached the outskirts of town. Time to face what could turn out to be the most devastating rejection of my life. My self-confidence was shaky.

Dick reached over and took my hand, squeezing it with positive energy. "It'll be just fine. You're following your heart and however it turns out, you are the strongest person I know. You'll handle whatever happens. I love you."

Tears trickled down my cheeks as outside the window everything blurred. "I couldn't do this without you, you know. I love you—more."

"No, you don't. I love *you* more!" His eyes crinkled into a smile as he asked, "So, what's the strategy?"

Wiping away my tears and blowing my nose, I took a deep breath, smiled back at him and said, "Well, I've been thinking about that. Let's start at the library. I'll introduce myself as an author doing research so we won't draw attention to her."

Pausing, I contemplated. "Ada. Ada. What a great name! Kinda rolls off my tongue. I like it. My mother's name is Ada. I'll see if I can find anything in old high school yearbooks. She must have graduated sometime between 1939 and 1941, so that's the place to start. Can you check out the farming section to see if you find anything on Walter or Matilda? The papers I copied on farming will be a decoy for the librarian."

"Sounds like a plan."

Medicine Lodge hadn't changed much. As in Pratt, our tires clunk-clunked over the bricks feeling as if they were square. The main drag gave the appearance of a sleepy cowboy town with about thirty stores; many with western style façades lined both sides of the street.

Parking across from the library, I stepped out of the truck, took a deep breath, and cautiously looked around, psyching myself for the next move. Dick held my hand as we crossed the street and opened the library's double glass doors.

219

"Hello, I'm looking for history on farming, and specifically anyone who might have graduated high school in the late '30's, early 40's and lived on a farm." I said to a neatly dressed, white-haired, red-lipsticked librarian.

"You'll find some of that information over here," she replied kindly, showing me to a cubicle with a microfiche machine. "If you need any more help, please let me know."

While I worked in the research area, Dick wandered by stacks of books and magazines on tables before checking the phone book for Ada M. Mitchell. No one listed by that name.

In the 1941 yearbook I found an Ada May Lillieqvist. My pulse quickened—and I let out a long slow breath while counting to ten in an effort to appear calm. Shit! I wished they'd included a photo.

Behind me, the librarian asked Dick "Are you finding everything?"

"No. Not yet," he replied.

"What is it you're looking for?"

"A woman named Ada Mitchell," Dick said, referring to a copy of Matilda's obituary we had obtained in Pratt.

"Oh. Ada lives right over here. Come with me." The librarian put her hand on his arm and led him toward the window. "See that white-and-gray pickup parked across the street? That's her house, number 113, just in front of that truck."

"That's her house" was all I processed. A raging red river pulsed in my chest, heartbeats surely heard throughout the library. Cemented to my seat, nothing moved but heart and lungs.

"Carol! Carol, come over here!" Dick urged, motioning me with his hand.

Slowly rising from the chair and feigning composure, I walked to his side, hooked my arm through the crook of his elbow to steady myself, and peered across the street, dazed. Incredibly, we'd parked in front of my mother's house. *Thank you, Universe! Thank you, Dream Woman!*

The librarian rambled on, telling Dick that Ada hosted Cultural Club until 4:30 P.M., but he should just knock on her door after that. "She's quite knowledgeable about these parts and I know she would be glad to talk with you. Are you a relative?"

Whoa! Had we blown our cover? Did I look like her? No, she'd asked Dick if *he* was a relative, not me.

"No," Dick replied. "We were given her name as a contact here in Medicine Lodge. Thank you for your help."

"Oh, she knows a lot about the area—and farming. You could call if you'd rather." The librarian wrote a number on a slip of paper. "Well, here's her number—good luck."

Thank God, Dick was able to respond. With all the aplomb I could muster, I sauntered back to the microfiche pretending to work as the screen in front of me blurred. *Oh, my God! She's alive. Please let her want to meet me. I don't deserve to be turned away after coming this far. Dream Woman, surely if this wasn't meant to be, it wouldn't have been so easy. She wouldn't reject me!*

Ten minutes later, Dick and I were sitting in our truck in front of Ada's house. Staring out the windshield, I whispered—as if speaking too loudly would disclose our presence, which I wasn't quite ready for—"My mother, my birthmother, is in that house. Right there in front of us. She's alive and well and hosting Cultural Club. We did it. We found her. Let's get out of here and find a place to stay."

Later, lying in the bathtub with water up to my neck, Dick parked on the flush, I said, "You've got to call her. What if she doesn't want to meet me? What if, by hearing my voice she feels obligated or weird or something? I don't want to influence her in any way, or cause her to feel guilty if she doesn't want to see me. It wouldn't be fair to her."

Silent, lips pursed, Dick rolled his eyes, his brow creasing, and looked at me.

"Don't look at me like that," I told him. "I'm not chicken! It's really important to respect her feelings. I can't hurt her, or worse, scare her away."

Dick's brow wrinkles deepened, eyes cast downward, his mental wheels turning, as I waited patiently. "Okay! I'll call her. What do you want me to say?"

After we rehearsed several speeches, I wrapped myself in a towel and anxiously perched on the edge of the bed while Dick dialed her number.

Four rings.

"Hello. Ada Mitchell?" Dick swallowed hard. His strong voice laced with Maine accent cracked slightly as he said, "My name is Dick Wyman. I'm here in Medicine Lodge with someone who believes she's a daughter you gave up for adoption many years ago. She would very much like to meet you, but if you feel you can't see Carol Ann, she would understand."

I heard a gasp, as Dick purposely held the receiver away from his ear, and my eyes widened.

"The Lodge Inn Motel," Dick said, nodding. "Yes. Overnight."

A long pregnant silence filled the room as Dick held the phone close to his ear. I sat frozen on the edge of the bed, knees drawn to my chest in a tight pyramid, my breath sucked in so deep my chest expanded by two sizes.

"Ayuh."

"Ayuh, ayuh," Dick grunted again, head cocked to the right, holding the phone with his shoulder now as he fumbled with the note pad on the table. "886-3080, room 224."

Then placing the phone in the cradle he held his arms open. I lunged into them.

"She wants to see you but she needs some time. She'll call us back in about half an hour."

My whole body shook while Dick held me tighter and kissed the top of my head.

"It's okay," he said. "She wants to see you, honey. She just needs time to catch her breath, too, I suppose. Either that or she's calling the cops."

"Oh! My God! Didn't she believe you? Does she really, really want to see me? Did it sound like she was excited or like she was saying, 'I *guess* I can see her'?"

"No, she really wants to see you. She sounded excited." He soothed.

"I did it. We did it! She wants to see me! This is finally happening. This is so…so…too, too much." I danced around the room.

Waiting was difficult! I took another bath while willing the phone to ring. This time Dick had a drink in his hand as he sat on the flush.

"What do you think was going through her mind?" I asked. "Did she say anything about wanting me to find her? Do you think she might not return the call? Tell me again what she said to you. What was her tone? Did she sound pleased? Scared? Suspicious?"

Laughing, he repeated for a second and third time exactly what Ada had said to him. It was like one of those stories children demand to have repeated over and over, even though they've heard it so many times they could tell it themselves.

Frowning, I said, "Maybe she'll be funny looking, not at all like me, more like Margaret with buck teeth and moles all over—another Polka Dottie." We broke into fits of giddy laughter.

When the phone did finally ring it startled both of us. Dick answered and gave me the thumbs-up gesture. "Of course we can. Whatever is best for you." Nodding and smiling, he went on, "Ayuh, ayuh. We'll be there at 8:00. I know the house. We saw it earlier today. Okay, goodbye."

223

I jumped up and down on the bed. Dick joined me but, after bouncing once and hitting his head, decided he'd better not try it again. After all, he stood six foot one and weighed 225 pounds.

"It's only six o'clock," I said. "What are we going to do till 8:00? Oh, I'm gonna call the kids right now!"

The next hour went by quickly while I called John V, Laura, and a few friends. Everyone was excited, asking for another call after our visit with all the details. Dick called his family too, who were equally excited.

At 7:45 I was pruney clean, dressed, and ready to meet my birthmother.

Parking in front of her house in the same spot as earlier that day, Dick leaned over and kissed me, then squeezed my hand like he was pressing the last drop of water out of a sponge, transferring confidence from him to me before I opened the truck door. Breathing deeply, my stomach flipping about like a fish out of water, I inched up the concrete walkway to my mother's house.

*My mother's house. My* mother's house. I wished someone could record every single thing I felt and saw exactly as I experienced it.

What did I want from my mother other than to see her, hear her voice, and know her history? I'd never fantasized a relationship. So I wasn't sure what to expect from either of us as I approached the concrete steps leading to the door. Sensing Dick close behind, my gaze was fixed on the door. It opened.

There, framed by the doorway, yellow light streaming from behind her, stood a short woman slightly heavier than me with outstretched arms.

Her face was square, skin smooth and creamy— with no moles—brown eyes wrinkled like crushed tissue paper at the corners and the brightest fuchsia lipstick I'd ever seen.

"Welcome."

As I stepped forward she pulled me into an embrace. It wasn't a hello nice-to-meet-you-pat-the-back, or God-it's-good-to-see-you-it's-been-a-long-time embrace, but a full body, no-holds-barred, you-are-my-lost-daughter hug. In those forty-five seconds of arms to arms, breasts to breasts, neck flesh to neck flesh I felt fifty-five years of prayers, tears, hopes, and fears transform into joy for this white-haired woman—as for me, I experienced a new level of gratitude.

Ada then pushed me a short arm's distance from her and looked directly at my face as if she was a detective, wielding a magnifying glass over important evidence. Soft brown eyes scanned my face and we sized each other up, both hoping to see similarities and flaws alike, turning what we'd visualized into its own truth, righting the wrongs of our fantasies, slowly seeing the differences.

Sniffling and swallowing, she said, "You know, the hardest thing I ever did was give you up." Then her trapezoidal mouth—surrounded completely by fine-line wrinkles that had taken a lifetime of smiles to create—opened into a Christmas-card-singing-angel oval as she gazed heavenward, then drawing out Oh as if she were pulling a bow across a violin string rising the pitch at the end with a squeak, she said, "Ohhhh, Momma Tillie, you have your blue-eyed girl!" Again she pulled me to her breast, almost smothering me, tears wetting my neck, stiff hair tickling my nose and smelling of hair spray.

Realizing that Dick was still standing behind us, we dragged him into our hugging circle. Ada grasped my manicured hand with her soft arthritic one and led me to the sofa where we sat, touching hand to hand, thigh to thigh. Dick sat opposite, observing us while Ada talked.

Listening intently, my eyes wandered, taking in the mostly blue living room. We were seated on a very long blue brocade divan that dominated the room, complemented by two upholstered chairs that were also blue. Adorning the walls were assorted paintings of robust women and country landscapes in thick swipes of earthy toned colors, gilded mirrors, and a host of framed pictures. A large wooden bureau and several curio cabinets with glass doors held blue china, crystal, a set of gold silverware, and other family memorabilia. Perhaps Ada needed something to do with her hands, or just presumed I would be curious about my ancestry, but she took out several photo albums, slowly turning the pages telling me about each of her siblings and parents, my relatives—just faces to me at this point—saying what a rich heritage we came from. How strange that sounded! *We came from.* How could she have known this was what I'd been seeking? A connection to family and the person or persons I actually look like. Whose characteristics had I inherited, whose habits, whose idiosyncrasies? I listened intently to the gravelly smoker voice coming from the trapezoid mouth, trying to absorb who all these people were, to place them in the correct sub-group within the gigantic world of this family and hoped to understand how all this fit into my own identity. This white-haired fuchsia-lipsticked lady held the key.

We didn't closely resemble each other, which appeared important to her—just as it was to me— because she kept asking Dick if he saw a likeness. Nor did she fit the vision of my Dream Woman.

She talked non-stop, lower lip opening and closing as if tied to strings manipulated by a puppeteer, or a post, reminding me of a marionette—square jaw, mouth open, close, open, close. *Was this nerves or her usual way?* When she smiled the thin-lipped trapezoid transformed into a pink up-turned smiley face big enough to hold a whole doughnut all at once. Whether or not she ate, or even liked, doughnuts I didn't know but it would have been fun to see if she bit into one or just popped the whole thing right in.

Overwhelmed, I smiled and nodded appropriately but retreated to a safer place in the recesses of my mind until I was able to be in Ada's presence once again, her realness my reality.

"Carol Ann, we're fortunate we come from a long line of accomplished and wonderful people."

Turning to Dick she went on, "I'm so glad you made that phone call tonight. You know, when my sister Vera got the internet I'd asked her to help me find my daughter, but we didn't know how to go about it, so I just kept praying that someday, before I died, I would meet Carol Ann. Anyway. You know, that's the name I gave her. When I heard you say her name, I knew instantly my prayers had been answered."

2000 - 2001

## Swapping Secrets

12 December 2000 – Medicine Lodge

Expecting to sleep fitfully, I was nicely surprised when the next morning I woke completely rested and energized.

Ada May Lillieqvist Mitchell turned out not to be the woman in my dreams, though finding her made her the woman *of* my dreams. But the Dream Woman dream continued to be part of my nocturnal life. Who was she? Surely not just some figment of my imagination!

The realization that Ada was not the Dream Woman was certainly not in the forefront of my mind as I spent that first evening with her. How could it have been? But at some point, I thought about the Dream Woman and took a hard look at Ada. I just didn't see it. Ada was not she.

The following morning, as I walked around my mother's home, family memorabilia took on new meaning. *How unfamiliar that sounded.* Those thick stroked oil paintings and sketches were those of her paternal grandmother, Adelé Lilljeqvist. In a hutch, she kept silver and china from the Bernerhof Hotel in Berne, Switzerland, which had once belonged to her great-grandmother Constance Wieland.

My, how proud Ada was of all the Lillieqvists and their lore. She rambled on and on about her sisters, parents, grandparents, aunts, uncles and cousins—a whole host of Lillieqvists. This was the gift she'd wanted to bestow upon me.

"See, Carol Ann, here *is* your legacy. This is who you come from. I'm so glad you're here now so I can share all this with you!"

I'd been living for this moment. I'd loved all my grandparents, the McCallums, Russells, and Richardsons (even though I'd only met the Richardsons a few times), so had only tasted what it might be like to have a long-term grandparent relationship—a legacy. Certainly nothing the likes of this large family!

As we sat at the small table in Ada's red-and-white kitchen eating breakfast, I asked about her life in Kansas.

Growing up on the farm, she'd milked cows and helped her family work the land. Her father's unique way of terrace farming, which he'd learned in Switzerland, allowed him to do well as a farmer. He and Tillie had been active in 4H, involving their children at every opportunity. Gaining renown, Walter had taken a leadership role in farming by experimenting with different methods of crop rotation. Pulling me out of the chair and practically dragging me into her garage, Ada pointed to the Skelly Foundation Award hanging on the wall. Puffing out her chest, she squeezed my hand saying, "Within our modest community, my parents were looked upon with respect, and when all is said and done, that is a great thing to strive for. It's something I've tried to pass along to my children."

Her voice thick, eyes wetly glistening, she said, "You know, in 1927, when Dad went to Bern to see Adelé on her deathbed she told Swede, that's what we called Dad, that she was bequeathing him money and he was to go home and build a nice house for his family on the land in Kansas. That's how we got the new brick home I grew up in. Anyway." Opening her mouth wide she stuck out her tongue emphasizing the strong emotion she felt—a strange habit, and one I would come to understand and love.

Back in the kitchen, she carried on, speaking of her five siblings and what a close-knit family they were. Ada shared funny anecdotes, laughing at herself wide-mouthed and slapping the air. She recalled the time she'd gotten caught in the basement opening jars of canned peaches, tasting each one to decide which she liked the best, and how one day when her mother went to town for groceries, she'd put on Tillie's white high-heeled shoes and broken a heel. Knowing she'd get in trouble, she'd placed the shoes back in the closet, positioning them as if nothing was wrong. Hmm, this sounded similar to something I might have done.

Frequently swallowing rising emotion, and shrugging her shoulders, she told of her family's difficulties during the Depression and World War II. Despite the hard times, they'd managed to send her to college where she endured severe homesickness. She'd returned home soon after leaving, only to be fussed over by her mother and then lovingly, but firmly, taken back by her father. She successfully obtained a lifetime teaching certificate which, given the time period and her gender, had been quite an accomplishment.

During the war, dancing offered entertainment and Ada had enjoyed going to the USO with her girlfriends. It was there she'd met my father. Ada confirmed what the agency had told me about him, but didn't add much else. Like me, she'd disassociated herself from the shame and truly didn't remember. "Your father and I shared good times together. A friend told me he was married, so I broke it off. He didn't know about you, Carol Ann. I only learned I was pregnant after we'd broken up," she said, doing the open mouth, protruding tongue, shrugging thing again.

That my father hadn't known about me didn't bother me right then. Perhaps it meant one less person to search for or emotionally connect with; perhaps this huge Lillieqvist family was more than enough. Of course, I'd been curious about him but understood when she couldn't remember the father of her baby. Hell, neither could I. "Tell me what you do remember, Ada."

In her now familiar drawn out Oh, she reminisced,

233

"Ohhhh, he was handsome, a good dancer, a flyboy, and an undertaker. That's about it." Then she slapped the air dismissing any further discussion on the subject. A flyboy. A risk-taker just like me. *Was he a flyboy first, then an undertaker? Or vice versa? Why would anyone want to be an undertaker? Was that a family business or something that interested him? Did he see the draft coming and join, becoming a pilot to avoid footslogging? Which branch of the service was he in? Didn't the Navy and the Air Force both fly planes?* All questions for future answers!

Ada skipped lightly over her pregnancy, saying she had lived in the moment and moved on, keeping her secret and not letting it cripple her. But she enthusiastically told us of her nanny job—after having given me up—for a wealthy family in the Hamptons that lasted about a year until, again missing family, she'd returned to Kansas to teach in a one-room schoolhouse near the family farm.

"Little Bobby Mitchell was one of my first grade students. He took such a shine to me and one day he'd simply announced, 'My daddy is going to take you out on a date.'" I didn't know whether to take him seriously or not, but Jim Mitchell called later that week. We enjoyed one another's company and soon one thing led to another."

Jim was a widower with two small children, Bobby and Martha (nicknamed Marty). On Christmas Eve 1948, Ada and Jim Mitchell were married in front of the fireplace in her family's farmhouse.

The young lovers ranched, working side-by-side. Carving out a life for themselves on the Kansas plains, they were actively involved in their community. Ada raised Jim's kids as her own, but they'd never had children between them and she hadn't regretted it, although she'd often wished she would one day meet her only biological child.

She and Jim lost everything in a fire in 1965, but the biggest sadness for Ada was the loss of family memorabilia. Here again her determination and positive attitude showed. Tears fell from her eyes as she went on, relating how hard it was in 1993 when Jim passed away. They'd had a good life together and she still missed him, physically expressed by the now familiar tongue-shrug habit.

That morning in her Kansas kitchen we discovered a host of moments in our lives when we'd almost met. Ada and Jim had indeed been actors in the Peace Treaty reenactment I'd attended. Marty's husband, Mike, and their daughters Raelyn, Amber, and Robin, (my nieces) had attended Northwestern Oklahoma State University in Alva. Robin had been there during my senior year. Wow! Dr. Floyd Sibley the sociology professor for whom I'd written the independent-study adoption paper turned out to be a family friend and his son Ron, a preacher, had presided at one of her family member's weddings. While I was living in Woodward, Oklahoma, Ada and her grandchildren had stayed at the Holiday Inn on several occasions, swimming in the pool and shopping at Wal-Mart, a special treat for rural kids in the '80s. We might easily have stood next to each other in the checkout line.

My mother had lived a mere 110 miles from me for eight of my twelve years in Oklahoma. Had I been brought to Oklahoma for reasons other than John's job?

I wanted to ask so much more, to know her story as it related to me. Like so many adoptees, I wanted to know why she'd given me up and what it had been like for her being single, pregnant, and living in a strange city so foreign to where she was raised. None of these were medical or health-related questions. Instead, they were questions that tug at basic human curiosity.

I wanted to ask those big questions, yet I held back. This was an overwhelming event in both our lives, and we needed to go slow, respecting each other's vulnerabilities. I was afraid of offending Ada and worried about how she might react to what I had to tell her. I didn't know her well enough yet, and I felt like an explorer on *Animal Kingdom*, sneaking up on some rare bird, fearing the slightest wrong move would cause it to fly away and never be seen again.

I wondered, as we viewed those picture albums, how she had found it possible on such short notice to take me in the previous evening. Had my own son come calling in such a manner could I have gotten my act together in only a few short hours and been the calm and gracious hostess she'd been? Ada Mitchell was a piece of work!

And then she breached the wall. "Carol Ann, were your parents good to you? Did you have a good life?"

She had to ask. I'd known she would. Here was one of the hardest things *I'd* ever have to do—as hard as giving up my own child, as hard as admitting to my sometimes shameful past, as hard as divorcing John. I'd rehearsed in my head most of the night, but it still took all my inner strength—and just the right words—to tell my mother, who gave me up in love, that my adoptive parents were abusive.

Glancing toward Dick for encouragement, I took Ada's weathered, arthritic-fingered, hands in mine and softly gazed into her brown eyes, "My childhood was rough, Ada. The early years were very good, but by the time I reached middle school my adoptive parents had abused me physically and emotionally. At sixteen, they locked me out of our house telling me never to come back. Eventually they disowned me. I wish it hadn't been that way, for your sake."

Lips pressed together tightly, her jaw muscles quivering, tears spilled from my mother's eyes as I attempted to squeeze love and forgiveness into her worn hands.

"Please don't feel guilty for the decision you made to give me up—or pity me. You need to understand I'm grateful for my experiences; they've made me brave and strong, a survivor of adversity. I not only came by those strengths from living life, but *you* gave them to me genetically. You are a wonderfully strong lady and I'm proud to be your daughter. I'm so happy we've found each other."

"Carol Ann. I'm so sorry!" she sobbed as Dick gathered us both into his strong arms.

Ada sniffled, blew her nose, and shrugged, twisting her shoulders at the same time. "I am so sorry you didn't have the life I wished for you but I am very glad you found me." Then she slapped at the air as if dismissing the past and said, "Well, anyway." (I soon learned this meant, time to move on.)

And so I moved on to the next disclosure—sharing how, like her, I had given up a child for adoption. Having walked in her shoes, I didn't harbor any anger or resentment—in spite of what Margaret thought.

I gave a quick synopsis of how I'd traveled the country like a gypsy-hippie, been adopted again, gone to nursing school, married, birthed John V and adopted Laura, divorced, met Dick, and ended up there in her kitchen. Whew!

The next day, before heading back to Colorado, I photocopied every picture and piece of information I could that concerned her parents and grandparents, knowing I'd want to study them—assimilating this wonderful heritage into my identity at my own pace. One of the items I copied was the Lillieqvist family tree. For the first time I knew my true family roots. In grade school when we'd had to trace our family tree, it had been a painful exercise for me. Teachers don't realize the impact this has on adopted children. They simply say, "Just do your adopted tree," not understanding that this statement validates not who the child is but who she or he isn't. From this point on, I would know to whom I belonged and how to answer those awful family-history questionnaires at every doctor's office. No longer would I need to avert my gaze, saying, "I was adopted. I don't know my family history."

From here on in, faces would belong to names on a real family tree and those faces would have meaning. I'd walk a little taller, hold my head a little higher, and smile from a deeper place when asked all those unintentionally hurtful questions.

Stalling our departure, delaying us as long as possible, Ada insisted on showing us her town. She drove around Medicine Lodge, giving a running commentary, until finally she came to a stop at the cemetery where her parents were buried.

Reverently standing before their resting place, shoulder touching shoulder, I wished I'd known them in person. But clearly that would happen vicariously through my mother and my new family. Again, struck by what a large part family played in her life, I was anxious to experience it as well. If only she would let me.

## Aunts, Uncles, and Cousins

12 December 2000 – Medicine Lodge, Kansas to Dillon, Colorado

Our ten-hour drive home provided ample time to begin processing the last day and a half. Before Ada had opened her door, in the forefront of my mind was potential disappointment if I found her deceased—or fear of rejection if she didn't want to see me. I'd been counting on Dick to act as a King's man—to put me back together should I fall like Humpty Dumpty—and had looked to him for validation of this surreal adventure.

Now my focus changed. How would this new relationship with Ada develop? It was as if on December eleventh, Ada had opened her heart and I was born all over again. But I had no room for a full-time parent or mothering-mother in my life. What I wanted was a mother with whom I could have an adult, interdependent relationship and who provided a connection to my ancestry.

"Honey, I hope Ada and I can have a good relationship, be more like sisters living separate lives, and seeing each other when we want to. I don't want her in my face all the time and I don't want to be in hers either. I hope she won't want to run my life."

"You'll be fine," Dick countered. "She seems grateful just to know you. I don't think she'll expect anything you don't want to give."

I'd protected my birthmother's privacy by using the façade of an author but I hadn't given any consideration to how my being her secret would affect how I'd feel about myself. Ada wasn't ready to disclose my adoption to anyone other than her immediate family. Although part of me understood her wish to maintain the secret, another part felt ashamed—ashamed for her, and for me. Would we ever be able to put these feelings behind us?

12 January 2001 – Journal entry, one month after Ada

Ada called this morning, crying. Yesterday she'd gone to Joanne's (a close family friend) and told her about me. Last night she hadn't slept well. Kept thinking about me, crying, feeling guilty over how "bad" my life had been, wishing she could have kept me, given me a better life, wishing she could have taken away the hurt.

11 March 2001 – Three months after Ada

Ada and I spoke on the phone at least two to three times a month now and were becoming more comfortable with each other. My kids would be with Dick and me for spring break, so I invited her to come to Colorado in April to meet her grandchildren.

With encouragement from her family, Ada slowly warmed to the idea of gently sneaking her secret out of the long-locked closet. Dan and Jean McKay, current owners of the Lillieqvist farm, were friends with all of Tillie and Swede's children, and particularly with Ada. Learning of our reunion and the planned trip, Jean offered to drive Ada to Colorado.

Excited and little nervous about having another grandmother, John V and Laura rose to the occasion, welcoming her as she had me in Medicine Lodge. Watching her interactions with my children, I was quietly pleased that she treated them both equally; and Ada was pleased when Laura said, "She's like a real grandmother. She brought cookies."

The second morning, over breakfast, Ada gazed up at the nearby mountain dissected into patterns of green and white with swatches of corduroy sometimes dotted with upside-down-canoe-shaped humps carved by tail-swishing skiers. "Carol Ann, do you think you can teach me to ski?"

"I'd love to." She was a seventy-seven year old Energizer Bunny.

Outfitting her in some of my ski clothes—which fit surprisingly well—we headed for the ski area. It took a long time to get the rental boots on and both of us got tickled, laughing when I forced her feet into them, grunting with the effort.

She slapped the air laughing and said, "Ohhhh, Carol Ann, you grunt just like our old farm pig." The biggest obstacle of the whole experience for her was walking in the boots. She looked like a two-year-old in Daddy's oversized work shoes. Once on the hill, I had to practically pick her up and carry her onto the magic-carpet that took us to the middle of the beginner's slope. Skiing backward with her hands tightly gripping mine, I guided her down the hill as *she* now mimicked a pig, squealing excitement.

"Carol Ann, this is such fun. I remember Swede telling me stories about skiing in Switzerland. This is so slippery!"

After two sweat-producing trips down the hill, she announced she needed to pee. Laughing at the thought of struggling with all the clothing again, and doing her tongue-shoulder gesture, she said, "Now I know what my dad was talking about, but his clothing was a lot easier to get in and out of. I think I'm done, Carol Ann."

Over the next four days, Ada shared stories of growing up in Kansas and questioned the children about their other grandparents, school, hobbies, and friends, wanting to know everything.

One evening, bundled against the cold, we all climbed into a gondola, giggling and joking as we ascended North Peak to the Alpenglow Stube restaurant. Exchanging snow boots for pre-warmed sheepskin slippers, we ordered elegant meals and listened to Ada tell stories of Switzerland and her father. She had a way of animating a story that captivated her audience and kept us in stitches.

I couldn't have asked for a better new mother.

16 June 2001 – Six months after Ada

Annually, the Lillieqvist siblings met for a family mini-reunion. Some years they would gather in Kansas, others they'd travel somewhere special; still other times, they would spend a week at one sibling's house, then caravan to another's, adding a family at each. Every ten years or so, they would hold a larger gathering for all the Lillieqvists, including the European branch.

Ada invited me to join her for a variation on the caravan version in June, which would provide her the opportunity to introduce me to the immediate family. The plan was to start with sisters Laurene and Corlena in Wichita, then brother Lucky would join us back in Medicine Lodge, and a few days later Ada, Laurene, and I would drive to Pearl and Orville's Wyoming home where Vera and Bob from California would rendezvous with us. Double whew!

Having rushed into each other's arms the previous December, we now strolled into our relationship incrementally, which felt right. After all, family was so central for her and I certainly didn't have a good reference point for that. Naturally excited at meeting these people, I was also apprehensive. In fact, had I met all these relatives that first day, it might have made me run in the other direction.

I peered out the window as though I was a young child flying for the first time, and felt as excited as if it was Christmas morning. When the plane touched the tarmac in Wichita and taxied to the gate, I searched the terminal windows for two short white-haired women. Ada's oldest sister Laurene—the only person to know that Ada was pregnant with me in 1945—would be accompanying her. No amount of deodorant, certainly not Secret, kept me from wetting the underarms of my blouse.

Spotting them right away in the small crowd just past the security station, they looked like two peas in a pod. Laurene smiled then pulled me to her enveloping me, which immediately settled the butterflies flitting about my stomach.

Our first stop was at Marty's home. I greeted her politely, if also tentatively, "Hello, it's so nice to finally meet you." What could I say? *Hi, I'm your new sort-of sister? I hope you don't mind sharing your mother with me?* Like Ada, Marty readily accepted me as part of the family, hugging me and introducing her children and grandchildren.

Six months earlier, in the red and white kitchen, Ada had told me to call her Mom, but I still wasn't comfortable doing that. I needed her daughter's permission as well, so taking Marty aside, I asked, "Marty, Ada said I should call her Mom but I'd like your opinion on that. After all, she's been your mother a lot longer and you don't really know me. I don't want to call her that if you'd rather I didn't."

"That's fine," she said, reassuringly touching my sleeve, "as long as she's happy, it's fine with me."

"Thank you!" I said, hugging her.

Our next stop, on the other side of Wichita, was cousin Linda's, where I met Aunt Corlena, her children and children's children. The scene repeated over and over as more relatives gladly welcomed me into the family. Triple whew!

That night, Mom and I shared a motel room. Alone together for the first time since I'd arrived in Wichita, we acted like girls in a dorm on the first day of school, talking long into the night until sleep finally overtook us.

The next day, tired from having listened to Ada snore most of the night, I dozed in the backseat most of the way to Medicine Lodge. Uncle Lucky, his wife Jean, and some of Mom's closest friends came by for a "meet Carol Ann" luncheon the following day. This was becoming confusing—so many people and all their different relationships—but I wouldn't have traded it for anything.

Our whirlwind family tour now moved north to Cheyenne, Wyoming where, for the first time, I recognized some of my own physical features in Aunt Vera—our mouths and hairlines.

This was the first time on the trip that Ada seemed to really relax, and another delightful aspect of this family surfaced: a fabulous sense of humor. When young, the Lillieqvist children had been divided by age into two factions: big kids and little kids. Ada had easily assumed the role of ringleader among the big kids, even though Laurene was older, and they all fondly saw her as the bossy one. She'd often been the instigator of pranks and the one who laughed the loudest. From a sideline seat, I watched them sitting around the table wagging fingers at each other, slapping the air for emphasis, and laughing at their own childhood antics, like the time Ada's teacher picked her up and sat her down in a fluted waste basket to discipline her and her bottom got stuck in it.

The next morning, Aunt Pearl fixed breakfast without bothering to comb her hair. Mom laughed, "Pearly, you look hick'ed this morning."

"Hick'ed?" I asked.

"Ohhhh, it's a word we made up when we were kids. We made up a lot of words. It means something not very good, you know like messy or not put together right."

Another funny incident involved the kids putting on a show for the family. Ada had made "poor pitiful Pearly" walk out into the living room to perform, naked. Pearl came out and told the folks, "Ada made me do it." Ada had gotten in trouble for that prank, but they all laughed over the re-telling of it. As she went on to tell of the time Tillie set the outhouse on fire trying to smoke out a skunk, I concluded that Ada came by laughter and mischievousness naturally.

My new family was certainly closely knit, evidenced by the way they laughed, cried, and hugged each other as we said goodbye to Laurene and the rest of my aunts and uncles.

Somewhere in Nebraska, I asked, "Mom, tell me more about your dad. What do you know of his early childhood?"

"Well, I do have a paper that has an excerpt from a diary Miss Ernst (Walter's nanny) kept. It tells of him looking like he'd been beaten at birth with one eye bigger than the other, and of him being a little hellion right from the start. He never liked staying in his pram (baby carriage) and was always taking his socks and shoes off," she said, chuckling. "Ohhhh, once he was all dressed up in white to go somewhere and got into a pot of blackberries covering himself from head to toe in blackberry juice. Another time he put his younger brother Arvid in the bathtub with all his clothes on and turned on the cold water." We were both laughing now, Mom slapping the air.

"I guess mischievousness comes to us naturally then, eh, Mom?"

"We both got those genes, Carol Ann," she said, as she shrugged and stuck out her tongue, a twinkle in her eyes.

"Mom, tell me about teaching in a one-room schoolhouse."

"Ohhhh, it was fun—and challenging. I taught all the elementary grades. Older kids would have to help with the younger ones. It gave them a lesson in responsibility."

"Did you ever have trouble figuring out what to teach?"

"Ohhhh, yes, sometimes." Giggling, she said, "One day I just didn't know what to do. We'd finished one subject and I hadn't really prepared the next. Improvising, I made the kids go outside and lie on their backs, telling them to find animals or faces or shapes in the clouds. Then we came in and they had to draw or paint them. I got a lot of funny papers that day."

*I love to search the clouds for faces of animals and people. Once in a while, I even see my Dream Woman's face in them.*

Ada soon fell asleep, her snoring providing white background noise in a symphonic synchrony with the monotonous thump-thump of rubber going round and round, as I wondered, *Did I fall down a rabbit hole when I found Ada?*

## Ada's Trip

For years, friends had urged me to write about my life because they found it interesting. When I opened a fortune cookie in December of 2000, shortly after finding Ada, and read, "It's time to write your book, others will benefit from it," I took it as an indication of what my next adventure should be.

"What would you think if I wrote a book about my life?" I asked Ada.

"Ohhhh, Carol Ann, that is a good idea," she said, a smile in her strong, gravelly voice. "You know, I don't know anyone else who has experienced all sides of adoption like you have. It would be a unique story."

"You know, Mom, I would want it to not only be a good story, but would hope that it could inspire others. Encouraging them to dream big dreams—trust in their ability to manifest what they want, crayon-outside-the-lines like I have, be true to themselves, and take part in their own destiny."

"That's good, Carol Ann. You know, I'd like to write a book one day. Maybe Jean can help me with it. I could call it *Ada's Secret*." Mom's friend, Jean McKay, had just published *Tillie's Bridge*, an anthology of excerpts from Matilda's journals about life on the farm, telling of her experiences with their animals, the land and crops, hard times and easier ones and, of course, the antics of her six children and husband.

For me, journaling had become a way of documenting JV's babyhood and I'd kept it up over the years, which provided plenty of material. Little did I know it would take over a decade to bring a book to fruition.

Driving from Cheyenne that spring, Mom and I'd fantasized about our writings, even dreaming of seeing them made into a movie centered on adoption.

"Ohhhh, you know, Carol Ann, my friend Betty Jo and I thought we were going to be movie stars—cause Uncle Willie said so." Ada laughed in a little girl voice. "He saw us doing cartwheels and handsprings, putting on shows while he was visiting us on the farm and thought we would be good actresses."

It didn't surprise me to hear that Ada put on shows or liked to be the center of attention. With her distinctly positive outlook on life, she certainly was entertaining.

"Let's pinky swear, Mom," I said, extending my non-driving right hand. "I'll write my memoir and you'll be the movie star."

"Okay then!" she replied, linking her pinky with mine and slapping the air.

11 September 2001 - Nine months after Ada

Over the summer, plans developed for Mom to visit Maine. I wanted my chance to show *her* off to my family and friends and have her see where I'd grown up. Taking a wild-card chance, I asked, "Would you consider meeting in New York City instead of flying directly to Maine? I'd like to see if the Spence-Chapin people could fill in some of the gaps in my birth story mostly about Glenn and Margaret, but maybe about what you told them about my birthfather, too. With you there they won't have an excuse to withhold information. You don't have to decide today, just think about it, and let me know. If you say no, I'll understand."

Before hanging up she said, "You know, Carol Ann, your idea is a good one. Maybe they could jog my memory too. It was so hard...giving you up." She choked.

I was delighted—and grateful to her for agreeing.

She'd fly to LaGuardia, and we were to spend two days in the city before going on to Riverside, Connecticut where we'd start our New England odyssey.

With long-term renters in my log home, I now spent summers at Dick's house or in the little shed-cabin, which I'd moved to a new location on the property away from the main house. In preparation for Ada's stay, I'd been permanently enclosing the screen porch turning it into a dining area from where the babbling of the nearby brook could be heard. Precariously balancing a four-foot-by-six-foot picture window in my outstretched arms, I lined it up in the rough opening and gently pushed it into place just as the phone rang. *Shit, what bad timing!*

Dick's voice was frantic, high-pitched. "Turn on the television: We're at war!"

I did, just in time to see a plane crash into the World Trade Center's South Tower. Forgetting about the window, I sat on the floor in front of the television with the rest of the world watching in disbelief as the events of September 11, 2001 unfolded.

*Oh my God—JV!* He was supposed to be flying home from Portland, Oregon! Thank goodness for cell phones. Planes all across the country were grounded. He'd heard the news while on the train to the airport, so he'd turned around and gone back to his cousin's. Then he rented a car and drove home—a much safer option that day, even if it meant a four-day road trip.

I called Mom around noon, feeling a need to talk to family. Still in shock, we were both functioning robotically.

"It feels like the day they bombed Pearl Harbor. So unreal!" she said, her voice shaky with emotion.

We spoke frequently in the next few days. At one point I queried, "Are you afraid to fly? It's okay, you know, if you want to change your plans." I certainly didn't expect her to live in fear on my account. "We could do this trip another time."

"No! No! They should have things sorted out by the time I go. I can't control when I'm going to die. If it's my time, then okay. I'm still coming!"

On September 23rd, Ada and I met in New York City. Our hotel was full with volunteer emergency workers from all over the country, there to assist in the aftermath of the attack. That evening in the bar, we heard firsthand some of the gruesome stories of rescues—and failed rescues.

Both of us tossed and turned most of the night. A pall of sadness descended over us, accompanying a deep sense of loss—both personal and global.

The next morning felt like a *Twilight Zone* moment as our car crept across the Brooklyn Bridge—the skyline of lower Manhattan altered. So strikingly different!

Spence-Chapin Agency was fairly easy to locate.

"This isn't where I came all those years ago." Ada commented.

"They changed addresses back in the 1980s, Mom," I said, holding the heavy wooden door open for her.

An agency worker greeted and escorted us to a comfortable room where, after cordial chitchat, she began to review both our records.

Finally I hoped to see what had been hidden all those years. Ada gave the agency worker consent for me to know anything and everything. Unlike my last visit, this time I specifically wanted to ask about Glenn. Both Ada and I wanted a reason—or at least an excuse—for his behavior.

The worker referred to the record then read, "Your father showed none of the symptoms other men exhibited after returning from the service. He remained the same person as before and didn't appear nervous or restless." She went on, noting his boss concurred with the agency's view of him at the time: my father had been

fundamentally healthy when he returned from the
service.

This didn't give us much to go on, but it was
unusual for him not to have any symptoms considering
what I knew had gone on in the Pacific Theater during
the war—the atrocities men witnessed and were
commanded to keep quiet about. Had he been really
good at following those orders, burying the trauma only
to have it resurface in his treatment of me? Or had I
been right about him turning mean after he failed to
make full partner in the firm? Was the combination of
both too much for him?

Ada listened carefully too, as she hadn't seen any of
those documents since the '40s. In fact, she probably
hadn't seen them even then, since they were a
distillation of the agency's observations of her combined
with what she'd told them.

She accepted some statements, smiling with humor
at some comments, and disagreed with others—shaking
her head in embarrassment, with eyes downcast and
fuchsia lips pursed, during the parts of the story where
she now admitted she'd lied outright.

Most of us like to go through photo albums from
our pasts. We see our own faces, our clothing, the
people we're standing next to, and the settings, trying to
put ourselves back in those scenes, getting sense
memories from those particular snapshots in time. Yet a
pensive distance shadowed Ada's face—she was seeing
much more than a photograph with missing pieces.

No matter how secure we are, we all wonder what
other people think of us, what impression we are leaving
with the world at large.

During the process of writing this memoir, I had
returned to Hartford to read what they'd said about me
when I gave up my baby, and experienced the exact
same phenomenon. In a photograph you're subtitling
the picture yourself, acting as a personal photo editor.
But reading a report of someone else's observations, you

CAROL LILLIEQVIST WELSH

never come out looking exactly the way you saw
yourself. In some ways you're far more heroic than you
actually felt, while in others, you're embarrassed by how
poorly you came off.

I had a perspective that few others have. Having
also relinquished a child for adoption, I understood and
empathized with Ada about having blocked portions of
the event from her consciousness, and for having seen
herself differently from the way they did.

Those of us who have given up children for
adoption are part of an outlaw sisterhood. Pro-lifers
support us and yet they usually do so at a distance, for
we are still the "fallen women." They see us as morally
inferior to themselves—even if they might have had a
lot more sex with different partners than we did (but
were simply luckier), or think all sex is bad.

What someone goes through in relinquishing a child
is a trauma, plain and simple. Postpartum depression is
an often-discussed topic but it is never spoken about in
reference to women who have given up their children
for adoption. Surely, logic dictates that women who
have relinquished, or are going through relinquishment,
face a more traumatic psychological situation. Like other
women recovering from delivery, we're hormonal as
hell, but our situation has been compounded by guilt
and the trauma of having a baby taken from our womb
and then handed off, never to be seen again. Perhaps a
combined diagnosis of post-traumatic stress disorder
and postpartum depression should be considered, for
surely it is that.

So, how do we get through it? Looking at my
mother, I'd considered the question. Most of us manage
by compartmentalizing; forming a special metaphorical
room in our minds where we stuff our hurt and
memories, then bolt the door so it can never be opened
again.

I'd opened the door to John, Dick, my kids, and a
few others. But now, as I spent time with my mother, I

252

acknowledged I'd probably withheld certain sadness, since all I could now recall were *facts* and not the colors and emotions of those tenuous moments so many years ago.

The visit to Spence-Chapin left us both emotionally drained. Appreciating the sunshine, we sought a nearby coffee shop with outside seating. In self-defense, our conversation turned superficial and we discussed current events and the city. We'd need a few days before either of us could again expose those raw, suppressed emotions.

Ada had arranged for us to meet Uncle Lucky's grandson's fiancée and her mother and sister for lunch on Fifth Avenue. Mom seemed to have family or friends everywhere we went.

Our Eastern road-odyssey began in southern Connecticut. Excitement bubbled up as I introduced Ada to my New England family and friends: brother Harry and his wife Cyndi, Carolyn and Ted, Nan and Andy (the children's godparents), and "Uncle" Walter. Coincidentally, Ada and I both had Walter mentors in our lives.

I'd been a bit nervous about introducing Ada to Carolyn, as I didn't want to hurt in any way the woman who had done so much for me, but Carolyn gracefully welcomed Ada, first extending a warm handshake then pulling her closer for a hug.

"Thank you. Thank you for caring for Carol Ann." Ada choked out, brine blurring her vision.

Over lunch, I gazed at the tranquil turquoise swimming pool surrounded by shrubs bronzing from the turning season, and let my mind drift to earlier times with my second adopted family while Ted and the two women got to know each other.

Carolyn proudly showed Mom around their home, then settled us into the guest room for a nap before dinner and a delightful evening.

CAROL LILLIEQVIST WELSH

As we said goodbye the next morning, I felt overwhelming love for both my mothers. Ada took Carolyn's hand in hers, saying, "Carol Ann had a rough time with the McCallums but you certainly did a wonderful thing by taking her in and loving her the way you did. She turned out pretty good. Thank you!"

After a night spent with Nan and Andy, and another with Harry and Cyndi, we stopped for an afternoon visit with a cousin of Ada's.

Our final stop before home was Boothbay, Maine, where I introduced her to my former husband John and his family. Mom was particularly thrilled at meeting John's father, Pop, whom she'd heard so much about from my children.

Dick had planned a lobster feed and baked a fresh blueberry pie to welcome Ada to our home and give her a true taste of Maine.

"Ohhhh, this is the best pie I've ever eaten," Ada mumbled, a bit of blueberry escaping the left side of her mouth.

The event was also an opportunity for her to meet Dick's family along with our close friends. I wanted Ada to hear my foster daughter's adoption story so Lisa, Gail, and her new husband, Bob, were also there. (Gail and Doug had divorced when Lisa was eight years old.)

Most adoption experts and psychologists recommend telling children early in life that they are adopted. For Laura it had been easy. We'd discussed adoption a lot at home so she'd just grown up knowing her story and accepting it as normal.

With Lisa it had been more difficult. Gail had sat down with Lisa shortly before she started kindergarten to carefully and patiently explain that she was adopted. Gail and Doug thought if she were older she would be able to better understand the concept, so Gail hadn't been prepared for Lisa's reaction.

"So, you're not my mom?" she'd asked.

"No, I *am* your mother. I just didn't birth you."

254

"You're not my mom!"

"Yes, Lisa, I am your mother. You have been my daughter since birth. You just didn't come out of my tummy," Gail explained softly.

"You're...not...my...mom!" Lisa repeated a total of *six* times, becoming more and more defiant with each saying.

Despite her initial reaction, Lisa eventually warmed to the idea of having been adopted and again accepted Gail as her mother.

By eighteen, Lisa was troubled in school, had attended alternative education and toyed with drugs. She'd been in and out of relationships, and now was in the same situation her birthmother had been in. Being pregnant had sparked her interest in knowing that woman. With Gail's encouragement and support, they searched and fairly easily found the woman who had given birth to Lisa.

Gail made the initial contact, then a few weeks later, the two of them traveled to Oklahoma to meet Lisa's birthmother. Like my reunion with Ada, their meeting was exciting and difficult all at the same time. The two of them stayed a few days at Lisa's birthmother's home, sharing their life stories, getting to know each other, and watching each other's mannerisms.

Taking the role of conscientious observer, Gail at one point fondly commented, "Now I know where your attitude comes from, Lisa. That genetic make up is so strong in some people you just don't remold them, even with lots of good nurturing."

I could identify with both sides of Gail's comment. Lisa's way of being defiant reminded me of the chip on my own shoulder, the one that I'd challenged my father to knock off and to which Margaret always referred. And thinking of my own adoptive daughter, I understood Gail's acknowledgment that no matter how you nurture a child, some things you just can't change.

255

Lisa and her birthmother hadn't created a close relationship as I had with Ada. They talked by phone several times after the visit to Oklahoma, but hadn't seen each other since. A re-uniting—and the subsequent relationship that develops—really can go either way, depending on a variety of circumstances. No way is right or wrong and it's not for anyone else to judge.

For Lisa, at her age and in her circumstances, just meeting and knowing her mother satisfied her. She'd had more of a curiosity than a need for a relationship because her nurturing mother was right there, by her side, loving her through good times and bad.

Increasingly fascinated with the nature-versus-nurture issue, I searched for any characteristics in myself that might have been genetic by watching Ada. I am light sensitive and sleep with my head under the covers unless the room is completely dark; my mother does, too. I like to be right, in control; so does my mother. I possess a competitive streak, especially with myself, striving for perfection; my mother does, too. When sharing a lighthearted moment with someone, people say that I wrinkle my nose and shrug. I'd been totally unaware of this tic until, seeing us together, a friend pointed it out. Not obvious similarities, but certainly a link to family genes.

Some characteristics my mother bequeathed are wonderful gifts, and a few are not so desirable. We'll be talking and suddenly discover something we both have done or still do. One of us will say, laughing, "Guess I know where that comes from!"

One of the strangest aspects of our being reunited was how things changed for Ada, the woman who had kept me a secret for so long.

In a phone conversation about a year after meeting, Mom said, "It's so good to be able to tell my story. I kept my secret too long."

Now she'd become completely open. If we were together somewhere, she'd ask anyone she could find to snap a photograph of us together—then, handing over her camera, she'd tell this total stranger, "This is the daughter I gave up for adoption over fifty years ago, but now we're back together."

A lot of people gave us that "Aw, that's cute" look but sometimes I found it downright embarrassing. "Mom, please, these people don't want to know all of our business!"

I'd smile, proud but embarrassed by her lack of reticence. At times, when I embarrassed them, my kids felt the same way about me. But for me, it went deeper. I still hadn't resolved being a secret. Was this old shame rearing its ugly head again? I wanted to have some input into deciding with whom she chose to share this information because maybe then I'd get past it.

I hadn't inherited Ada's facial features. The differences were not so stark that we thought we couldn't be related; but still, it was a bit of a letdown. Perhaps that sounds petty, but when you're put up for adoption, growing up among people to whom you have no biological tie, a yearning for similar-looking people arises. To find those people would give you that ultimate sense of family and an insight into your true identity. Because the McCallums didn't give me a sense of family, and my son John V was the spitting image of his father and grandfather, perhaps I pined for it more than other adoptees. I took some comfort in knowing I did resemble Ada's youngest sibling, Vera.

Still, a small piece of me wasn't satisfied, for in a dark corner of my mind, I still hoped to find that Dream Woman of mine.

2001- 2008

New Challenges

December 2001 – One year after Ada

My career in ski instructing came to a disappointing and unexpected end during the winter of 2001.

Dick needed a break from ski teaching—and perhaps from me, too. Longing for a change he'd decided to bartend for the season in Florida where his parents spent the winters. Dick and I respected each other's need for independence and self-exploration—each of us doing things in our own way. Having a large clientele of returning ski patrons provided a good seasonal income for me, so I was fine with the plan to winter in Colorado alone.

The season got off to a good start with several families requesting my instruction over the holidays, but on December 31, things changed abruptly. On the trail leading to the ski lift, a guy a foot taller than me skied dangerously close to several children. When I skied up to him to point out how close he had come to the children and asked to see his pass, he began yelling at me in a fit of "skier's rage" and reached out, grabbing my helmet and ripping it off my head, wrenching my neck and damaging the joints. Fortunately there were other people around who pulled him off as he whipped me with his ski pole.

By the end of that season, plagued by pain and unable to comfortably carry ski gear—and desperately missing Dick—I was ready to go home.

Dick was ready, too! He'd wished he'd been in Colorado to support me through all the stress. "It's a

261

good thing I wasn't there. I'd probably have done something we'd both have regretted," he commented.

After our winter separation and what had happened to me, Dick proposed, "With Laura in boarding school and long-term tenants in your Bethel house, I think it's time you moved in with me."

Welcoming his love and protection, I put my place in Norway on the market and did just that.

Struggling all summer with intermittent aches and pains from the injuries, it became more and more difficult to keep up with my lawn care business. Talking with Ada on the phone one day, she commented, "You need to stop working like a man, Carol Ann. Can't you find yourself a less physically demanding job? Crawling under tractors at your age isn't good for you." As much as I hated to admit it, Ada was right. That fall, I sold the business.

Substitute teaching and working at a call center kept me busy, but without health insurance and a regular income I could count on, I felt like a caged tiger stalking prey I couldn't reach. Instead of enjoying part-time "early retirement," I found myself praying to the Dream Woman asking for guidance and daily direction.

December 2002 – Two years after Ada

Dick had always enjoyed cooking and had secured a job in the kitchen at Mt. Abram ski area for the winter while I subbed, worked at L.L. Bean's call center, and rehabbed my neck.

In April, while attending an end-of-the-season kitchen staff party, I wound up chatting with a colleague of Dick's who also cooked for a nearby residential boys camp in the summers. When discussing how much he liked the variety of seasonal work, he suddenly said, "Hey, you're a nurse, right?"

"Yes."

"My camp director is desperately looking for a nurse. He's running out of time—we start next month preparing for the season. I could call him and set you up to meet with him, if you're interested."

Next thing I knew, I was a camp nurse.

Not having used my nursing skills since the '80s when I was in Oklahoma, I was apprehensive about returning to the profession. But the camp job turned out to be a fun way of easing back into nursing and it met my needs without having to complete a costly and time-consuming refresher course.

Apprehension aside, I dove right into camp life, loving the outdoors and the challenges that came with a certain level of authority and autonomy. But soon I discovered that camp nursing was no longer just fixing booboos and giving hugs as it had been in the days of my favorite storybook nurse, *Cherry Ames*. Now children came to camp with a multitude of medications that had the potential for serious side effects. There were privacy acts, accreditation regulations, and liabilities to consider. Finding the infirmary behind the times in several areas—not the least of which was good record-keeping and up-to-date policies—I set about writing a manual, establishing procedures, and working much longer hours than I'd anticipated. Yet I was enjoying nursing again. Nothing was more satisfying than seeing smiling faces leave the Health Lodge after an injury or illness, and watching little boys grow into young men, soon-to-be-leaders in their own right, all within the extended-family environment of Camp Wigwam.

At the end of our regular seven-week season, Camp Wigwam also hosts Camp To Belong Maine, which is a branch of a national organization that facilitates siblings separated by foster care or adoption being together for a week of enjoyment, discovery, and reunion in a safe and supervised environment. Again I became involved with children touched by adoption—what an honor and privilege to participate with this special group of children.

That summer was bittersweet—Dick discovered a lump in his neck that turned out to be stage-four throat cancer. On September 10th, he underwent surgery followed by thirty-three radiation therapy treatments. The next nine months were difficult and challenging for both of us, and I was grateful I didn't have a full-time job so I could care for Dick through his illness. As spring greened the earth, buds swelled as did our outlooks and life took on new meaning.

Fall 2004

Recovered from his ordeal and back to work, Dick was anxious to move on. Selling his house in North Norway, we purchased a mobile home from his daughter on Pike's Hill just down the road from where Dick had grown up. This was a good arrangement for both of them, as Dick felt he had come full circle and Kim needed a larger place for her growing family.

While sprucing up the trailer, unfortunately I discovered it was riddled with mold. Dick's health issues aside, living there was no longer an option. Through my connections with the summer camp, I became aware of a nearby campground that was going out of business and auctioning off cabins so I bought a 14 by 30 foot one for three hundred dollars. We had it moved to the trailer site, then spent three months living in the garage while renovating the cabin into a small efficient log home, where I now enjoy a view from our kitchen window of rolling forested foothills and snowcapped Mt. Washington dominating the distant horizon.

However, securing a more permanent, non-seasonal job proved more challenging than finding the one at camp. Tired of only piecemeal paychecks, while caring for Dick the previous fall and winter, I had sent résumés and applications out to local hospitals, home-health agencies, and schools—looking for any job that would provide insurance and a regular income. Not having working in hospital nursing for twenty-seven years put me at a distinct disadvantage. On the other hand, being a risk taker, I was open to almost anything.

By June, I'd just about given up finding employment in my profession and was gearing up for another camp season when, out of the blue, the local hospital called. They were offering a part-time position—twelve hours a week—as the Perinatal Education Coordinator for the Obstetrics Department. Apparently the camp director's glowing recommendation had tipped the scale in my favor when he stated, "Because of Carol's organizational, professional, and people skills our camp's infirmary has moved into the twenty-first century." His recommendation was provisional though—he wanted his lead nurse back in the summers. Talk about being validated!

I couldn't have asked for a better setting in which to re-enter hospital nursing and teaching. I was again working with women who wanted to learn all they could about birth and being the best moms they could be.

CAROL LILLIEQVIST WELSH

Switzerland Bound

In 2000, when I'd read the account of grandfather
Walter's journey to Switzerland to be with his dying
mother, a fantasy was born. How awesome would it be
to see for myself where my ancestors had lived?
I'd shared with Ada how Walter's agricultural
college in Switzerland was a lead in my search for her
and how I'd love to see his school and the Hotel
Bernerhof of which she was so proud. Ada heartily
agreed that a trip was in order. But before we had a
chance to solidify our plans, she succumbed to several
maladies of age: a hip replacement here, a triple bypass
there.
Still, my European roots intrigued me. Grandfather
Walter had been born in London. Was that why I'd
always felt comfortable there—was it a genetically
inherited memory?
That my American-born mother corresponded so
frequently with her European relatives seemed special.
The Lillieqvist heritage was rich. They knew exactly
where they came from, could all name their great-
grandparents, great-great grandparents and so on, back
through the years, and it seemed to me it helped them
understand their own personal traits, their life interests,
and their talents.
"Why am I successful in business?" one might ask.
Someone else would offer, "Well, that might be
because of Uncle So-and-So, the great bridge builder."
These people might hold keys to some of my
unanswered questions.

September 2007

"Carol Ann, do you still want to go to Switzerland?"

"Are you serious, Mom? Of *course* I do!"

I'd almost given up hope of visiting our relatives with my mother, thinking someday I'd have to hop on a plane to track these people down by myself. Finally, she hit a stretch where her health was good enough to travel such a distance.

We planned a spring trip, ending the conversation with her saying, "Okay then. I'll write the cousins in Sweden and Switzerland."

January 2008

Why was it taking Mom so long to contact them? Could it be she was still ashamed of her secret?

The telling of a secret this big that'd been hidden this long was no easy thing, especially when it's family you've kept it from. Even telling a friend is easier, as shame runs deeper in families.

February 2008

"Carol Ann, write this down," Mom commanded, giving me phone numbers for both Swiss and Swedish relatives, then instructing me to call them. She had finally written and now having heard from them needed to solidify our plans. "I just can't find the time with all that I have going on with the Heritage Center."

Why couldn't she call? How would these people relate to me? I didn't know them. What was I supposed to say? *Oh, hi, this is Ada's daughter, the one she never told you about.* Thought I'd just call and see what you think of her having a secret like that? Oh, by the way, I'd like to see how you're going to treat me when she shows me off

267

to all of you. Good Godfrey, Mom—why were you
putting me in this position?

"Mom, have you spoken with them since you wrote
last fall? Do they know about me? Will we even be able
to understand each other? Do they speak English? What
am I supposed to say to them?"

"Ohhhh, yes, they speak English. Anders, my
Swedish cousin, is coordinating with your cousin Uele in
Switzerland. They're making the arrangements for
accommodations." Her tone now turned more defensive
then bossy. "I told them about you. Just introduce
yourself and give them the details of our trip. They're
very nice people. You'll be fine."

"Can't you call them, Mom?" I pleaded.

"Ohhhh, every time I try to call overseas the phone
doesn't work right. You do it. You're closer."

What kind of rationale was that? It didn't cost any
more to call from Kansas than from Maine, although
living on a small, fixed income she had reason to worry
about cost. "Mom, I'll send you a calling card. That way
you won't have to pay for it; you just have to dial the
numbers on the card. You can talk for as long as you
want."

"No, no, that's too complicated. You call, Carol
Ann!"

She didn't leave me another option.

March 2008

Procrastinating for as long as I possibly could
(three or four weeks), I called Mom back. "Can you give
me those phone numbers again? I've misplaced them."

Steeling myself while punching in Uele's numbers,
I secretly hoped no one would answer and an automated
machine would give me a hint about whom I might
encounter on the other end of the line. Waiting patiently
through eight or nine rings, I was just about to hang up
when a female voice with a foreign accent said, "Hello?"

"Hello, this is Carol Ann, Ada's daughter. I'm calling from America. I'm aware you don't know me and it's strange making this call, but Ada insisted," I blurted, as if spewing the small print on a product disclaimer. "I'm calling to confirm the itinerary for our trip," I continued, and then rattled off our flight information. *Whew!*

"Oh. Hello, Carol Ann, this is Margrit. We are so glad you are coming. The whole family is anxious to meet you. I don't know the details of your lodging accommodations but when Uele gets home from the office, I'll have him call you. That should be in an hour or so."

Later that evening, Uele phoned back. His soft voice soothed as we conversed easily. He and Margrit would meet us at the airport and all the cousins, Swiss and Swedish, were arranging our lodging and planning an itinerary between them. This wasn't so bad!

3 May 2008

Cousins. My oldest friend Nan was the closest thing I'd ever known to a cousin. Such a simple thing, cousins—and now I had them on both continents. Being part of something as large as the Lillieqvist family enthralled me.

Now sitting on a plane bound for Europe with my mother, soon to be eighty-six, and me sixty-two, I found it necessary to pinch myself to be certain I hadn't slipped into an alternate reality on this already surreal trip.

Asleep, somewhere in that place between twilight and REM, I dreamed.

*Walking along a riverside with a book in my hand, I hear my name called. Turning, I see a female figure hurrying to catch*

269

*up. As she gets closer, I recognize my Dream Woman. Her right hand tucked behind a thin waist, she holds out her left hand, gesturing for me to give her the book. As I place it in her hand, she offers me my old teddy bear from behind her back. Holding him tight, I gently rub my fingers over his worn skin.*

Waking with a start to find the flight attendant serving our meals, I absentmindedly put my tray table down while Ada ordered glasses of celebratory wine.

Over the meal, I asked, "Mom, when you gave me up, did you leave me a teddy bear?"

Her brow wrinkled and she turned her eyes upward, searching her memory. "No, I don't remember any teddy bear. I did go to Bonwit Teller's and buy you a little white dress with a bonnet that the agency was supposed to dress you in when they gave you to your adoptive parents. I don't know if they did that. But, no, I didn't give you a teddy bear. Why do you ask?"

"Just now I was dreaming about the panda bear I've had all my life. It was one of the few things Margaret left out for me when she and Glenn kicked me out. I thought it might have been you who gave it to me. Maybe I'd always just wanted to think it was something from you."

Her eyes looked downward and with a sad, wistful expression veiling her face, she said, "Well, I wish I *was* the one who gave it to you, Carol Ann."

Relatives and a Revelation

4 May 2008

Walking toward the terminal in Zurich, I anxiously scanned the faces of people waiting for arriving friends and relatives. Of course Ada would recognize her Uncle Erik's side of the family but I, too, wanted to see familiarity in that human sea.

My disappointment surfaced as Cousin Uele hugged Ada. His face was round, mouth trapezoidal like Ada's, but I saw no distinct resemblance to me.

Both he and his wife warmly welcomed me as if they'd known me all my life and chatted comfortably while they drove us to our hotel a short distance outside Zurich. Listening carefully, taking in every word but not wanting to seem overly eager, I looked out the window seeing tall, modern buildings give way to industrial warehouses and large box stores like *Ikea* and *Home Depot*. The landscape changed again—lush green hills with small villages nestled here and there.

Reaching the town of Wetzikon and our hotel, Mom and I were running on low batteries from the long trip and soon plopped onto our small, single beds "getting horizontal" for a much-needed anti-jetlag nap.

The telephone startled us awake, announcing that the next set of cousins, anxious to meet me, were waiting in the lobby to take us to their home for dinner.

Half-drunk from heavy sleep, we robotically dressed then hurried into the elevator. As the doors opened onto the lobby, I again secretly searched for reflections of myself. Mom's cousin Rudi, looked a bit like Uncle Lucky. He and his wife, Verena Lilljeqvist,

271

CAROL LILLIEQVIST WELSH

also welcomed me as if I'd always been part of the family. As we pulled into the parking area of their four-story tan and white condo, bright red awnings extending from some of the units, I saw a little boy jumping up and down waving a hand-drawn paper American flag in our honor.

Being introduced to even more relatives here was similar to my experience in Kansas several years earlier. But now I actually identified a few familiar characteristics in both of my direct cousins—a nose, and similar hands—evidence that I did indeed belong to these people and a wonderful feeling of inclusion spread though me like butter melting on warm bread.

Naturally they were as curious about me as I was about them, asking about my life and specifically how I had found Ada and what that was like for both of us. Then it was my turn to press them for family stories and ancestral facts.

I'd purchased a tape recorder just for this trip but had left it in the hotel. Now I wished I hadn't, for Verena possessed a wealth of knowledge about the Lilljeqvist history both in her memory and the memorabilia displayed in their simply furnished condo.

Sitting down to a meal of cheeses, meats, breads, and raw vegetables, the family questioned us further about our reuniting. Repeating the same story over and over was becoming tiresome, but as we got into the telling, neither of us could stop the excitement of that experience from bubbling up.

In spite of being dog-tired and sated by the meal, I noticed two landscape paintings done by my great-grandmother Adelé in her now familiar hand with its strong brush strokes and saturated colors. "Verena, did you know Adelé? What do you remember about her?"

"She was very devoted to her painting. I have a few photos of her and the children. I'll get them." Verena rose, retrieving a worn album from the shelf.

I turned fragile pages while Verena related how Adelé had started painting early in her life. At the age of twelve she took her first lesson. The painting method in vogue at the time was to use thin brushes and anxiously fine strokes, the finer the better. But Adelé soon became impatient and lost her temper, changing her thin brush for a broad one, which began a long career and the signature of her paintings. *Could this also be the source of my rebellious spirit?* A love for painting continued throughout her life and she studied under many famous artists. Without the assistance of her friend, Miss Ernst—who served as nanny for her five children—she wouldn't have been able to devote as much time to her beloved painting. Once renowned, Adelé had founded The Sanary School for Artists in that same town on the French Riviera.

The worn, dog-eared pages of the photo album contained pictures of Grandfather Walter proudly playing a cello and one of him sitting on a horse, very much like the one of me sitting on Caisson years ago at Bonnie Oaks. And one was a black and white photo of a painting that I'd seen before in my mother's house, of the five boys dressed in fancy sailor suits, berets atop their heads, ready for a journey to Sweden. As I turned the pages, Verena remembered stories about my grandfather's curiosity, a trait that got him into trouble at times, all of which I easily related to, nodding my head in unison with her telling.

Centered on the next page was a photo of a petite woman with white hair parted in the center, pulled away from her small face, and gathered into a loose bun. Wearing a dark collared dress, she was surrounded by six boys and a girl, all wearing sailor suits. They posed in front of a glass-paned door with leafy deciduous trees gracing the background. The woman had a dimple in the center of her chin, high cheekbones, and thin lips turned upward in a soft smile that wrinkled the edges of her eyes.

273

It was a typical picture, taken not with the owner's camera but by a photographer, perhaps for the family album, or to be sent out later in the year at Christmas time. Originally the edges would have been smooth, details crisp, but while aging on a shelf, the three by five paper had curled and faded it to somewhere short of sepia.

All this detail registered in my grey matter in just a fraction of a second before the room darkened, and I felt myself freefalling like a skydiver into a slowly swirling vortex. Descending deeper into the void, I wasn't afraid. In spite of the stomach-in-your-throat sensation I was feeling—the kind you get when dropping or rising quickly in an elevator—I felt protected. A face appeared out of the darkness and arms enveloped me. In that instant, an inner knowing that I can't explain permeated every cell in my body: I recognized the face at the end of this whirling tunnel as the one in the photograph—she was the woman of my dreams, my guardian angel and mentor. It was she who had held me close all these years. How long I remained detached from the scene at the table suspended in space was probably only seconds in reality, but felt timeless to me.

Verena on my left, Mom on the right, both reached out simultaneously, touching my hands and shoulders in comfort, puzzled and concerned by my behavior.

"Oh my, Carol Ann, what is it?" Mom asked. "Are you all right? Are you ill? Carol Ann!"

Their voices sounded distant, as if they'd called from the top of a mountain, the sound echoing in my ears, and that tight lumpy feeling you get when you know you're going to cry rose in my throat. Carol Ann, Carol Ann, Carol Ann. Salty droplets seeped from my eyes. Speechless, I pointed to the photograph with one hand fanning my flushed face with the other.

Minutes that must have felt like eons to the two women passed before I was able to choke out a whisper, "Dream Woman. That's my Dream Woman."

"Take your time, calm down. Here, blow your nose," Mom said, handing me a tissue.

Gaining some composure, I explained, "Ever since I was a teenager, I've had a recurring dream about a woman who comforts and guides me. She's helped me though a lot of tough times."

Sniffling, I said, "Mom, before we met I had fantasized you would not only be my mother, but the woman in the dream."

I reached out and touched the face on the yellowed page with the sensitive pad of my forefinger, gently caressing her, and said, "I look like my Dream Woman. Do you see the resemblance?"

Verena said, "Yes, I do, and it doesn't surprise me. That is your great-great-grandmother, Constance Wieland."

Reflections on Constance

Constance!

At times I'd related to her, as if I'd somehow been able to travel back in time, the old self speaking to and comforting the younger self. In my dreams, the Dream Woman was I and at times I was she. Yet that explanation never quite fit. My Dream Woman was a wise, separate entity, an elder—wiser than I ever expected myself to be.

Through Ada, Constance was my direct line to the past, to that thing we know as family.

I finally felt connected!

7 May 2008

Before dawn, thoughts were already butterflying through my consciousness. *I'm different from who I was yesterday.* Rising, I quietly tiptoed into the bathroom so as not to wake my mother and gazed into the mirror at my new reflection—a content woman with a soft radiance, a woman changed forever—and thought, *I am Carol Ann Lillieqvist.*

Mom stirred and stretched, then said, "Good morning, Carol Ann. How did you sleep?"

"OK, I guess." Then taking a risk, concerned I might have hurt her feelings the day before, I asked, "Mom, were you slighted last night when I discovered Constance was the Dream Woman?"

"Ohhhh, no Carol Ann." Then after a long pause, "Well, maybe a little, but it's okay. I'm glad you saw that photo."

Pulling her into my arms I said, "I'm sorry, Mom, I would never intentionally hurt you."

As we dressed for our day trip to Berne, pictures from the *Golden Book of the Grand Hotel and Bernerhof*—the book I'd seen the night we reunited—came into my consciousness. This once-grand hotel built by our relative, Jean Kraft, had been a place of legend within my family, the thing they were known for, the touchstone of their lives.

"Are you excited to go back to Berne, Mom?"

Smiling as she applied the finishing touches of make-up, she said, "Yes, I am. I can't wait to show you the grand hotel Constance owned. You know, one time when Jim and I were on a business trip in Switzerland, I went to Berne by myself and, by accident, was fortunate enough to meet the groundskeeper at Number 7 Gryphenhübeliweg. That's the house Dad lived in with Adelé, you know. The man even talked with the owner, arranging for me to go in the house. It was quite an experience."

While Mom would be reliving her last visit to this place ten years earlier, I would be seeing everything through the eyes of a new identity. Holding an image of Constance in my mind, I was still trying to assimilate the revelation of the previous night, and I hoped that maybe I would feel the ghostly presence of Constance today.

Driving along the A1 toward Berne, rich fields of newly planted crops and farmland dotted with healthy grazing sheep and cattle whizzed by my backseat window as I again half-listened to the front seat conversation. On the outskirts of Berne, Uele pointed out a cluster of white limestone and red brick buildings nestled into the hillside that were the Swiss Agricultural College Walter had attended.

My grandfather came into contact with kings and queens, presidents and potentates, people of all high stations by living near and playing in the family hotel with his mother and grandmother. It had not been royal birth, but a heritage of hard work and good business sense that had allowed all of them to rise to such levels.

Constance reportedly was responsible for Walter's tenure in America. By telling a hotel guest who owned a large ranch in Nebraska Walter's dream of becoming a farmer, one thing had led to another and before long Walter was headed for the United States to work as an apprentice. With a sponsor and a place to live already arranged, Walter hadn't needed to negotiate his way through Ellis Island: he'd simply skipped right on through to the American heartland.

How brave my grandfather was to follow his heart and come to America! It was a real mark of character to find a passion and follow it.

Walter worked on the X-Bar cattle ranch until he'd saved up enough money for the purchase of eight hundred and sixty acres of his own land in neighboring Kansas—a long way from Berne, which we were now approaching.

The old city dated from medieval times and still radiated a wonderful Middle-Ages flavor, consisting of stone buildings bunched closely together with red clay-tiled roofs. Two stone bridges crossed the Aare River, milky aqua from glacial melt-water streaming into it from nearby mountains. The river bent into a tight C with the old city tucked inside the curve. On the opposite hillsides sprawled modern city buildings and residential neighborhoods. Cobblestone streets slipped time backward.

The Hotel Bellevue was almost identical to the Bernerhof. Strolling through the vestibule, we stepped out onto an open-air dining terrace—La Terrasse—where tables covered with pink tablecloths and shaded from the bright mid-day sun by matching umbrellas contrasted with the turquoise Aare. Views led to fields of oilseed rape crops, blooming yellow and framed distantly by the snowy Alps with peaks like meringue topping.

The Bellevue put the "grand" in grand hotel with high multi-hued stained-glass ceilings in the lobby, chandeliers and marble columns, marvelous works of art decorating the walls, and red-carpeted staircases where one might expect to see a duchess descending in a flowing gown. Several rooms held finely upholstered chairs set in conversational groupings for high tea. But try as I might, I couldn't get Constance's image to come to me in this place.

Although the Bernerhof no longer belonged to any of us Lillieqvists or Lilljeqvists, I still hoped to see and experience it with old eyes, eyes that would travel into the past, imagining ghosts of proud ancestors lovingly breathing upon the back of my neck.

Finally, we all stood before the ancestral building. I marveled at the gray stone structure with its first floor of arched paned windows. Over the three similarly arched entry doors hung a glass portico providing shelter from the elements and leaving visible the trademark of Jean Kraft—three crown reliefs chiseled above the lintels directly over the grand doors. By the entry hung a shiny brass plaque stating the date of construction, 1855-1859.

Uele and I entered the building where a series of plain doors—instead of the gala foyer and drawing rooms of yesteryear—faced us. Approaching a glass window in the wall to our right, Uele spoke with the security guard in Swiss-German explaining our third great-grandfather had built this hotel and our second great-grandmother once owned and managed it. He asked, "Could we view any part of the building?"

Shaking his head the guard said, "*Nein. Nein.*" No tours. The building had been converted into government offices in 1924 and was off-limits to the public. I wished we could get inside but would have to settle for seeing what I could from the foyer and the outside.

Ada now joined us flashing her fuchsia smile at the guard in her most persuasive and charming way. "My father told us children many wonderful stories of growing up in this hotel, spending time with his grandmother. I'd really like to see where he played." Uele translated for her.

The guard's mouth creased into a smile as he motioned for us to wait with a palm outward. Soon a tall, stately woman arrived and after speaking with Uele and Mom, took us on a guided tour of the first floor. We were all elated and honored.

Our guide escorted us into a large hall. Crossing the threshold, I time-traveled to a scene from *The Golden Book*, to this same chandeliered hall in black and white, imagining gilded gold, sparkling crystal and elegantly dressed VIPs eating lavish food in honor of Emperor William II, served by formally dressed wait staff—all managed by Constance. Before I could daydream any further, we were hurried out onto a veranda with a similar view to the Bellevue's but with one difference. Here, below the stone balcony, a stately group of chestnut trees grew adjacent to a lovely courtyard where my grandfather had played as a young child.

These trees were not simply trees: they were the *same* chestnut trees under whose boughs my grandfather had amused himself. The building itself was not simply an old building, but one that my ancestors had built, owned, and dedicated their lives to maintaining. When people talk about the family homestead, well, this was mine.

Intricate handcrafted crown-molding, ornate reliefs over doorways, and large arched windows with lacy curtains graced the rooms. I flitted back and forth between present and past, sensing the family ghosts I'd so wanted to conjure up, imagining Constance leading us through her hotel rather than the Swiss government worker.

280

Our guide was so taken with our family's history that she bent the rules to include a special visit to the basement. During government renovations in 2004 and 2005, the central courtyard was dug up and workers had found the gravestone of Jean and Eduard Kraft (Jean's son and Constance's brother.) As the basement elevator doors opened, the relocated gravestone faced us, mounted on a remnant of the original medieval town wall.

*Here in rests in the peace of our Lord, Jean Kraft, Founder of the Bernerhof, Born 27 January 1809, Died 12 October 1868, Eduard Kraft, Born 10 December 1849, Died 8 February 1924*

As I looked at the screen on my digital camera, Ada posed for me, all puffed up with family pride in front of the mounted gravestone. Gooseflesh rose on my arms and a shiver ran down my spine as, in my imagination, she became her father running through this grand hotel, then Constance graciously greeting nobility—and I suddenly realized I too was not only myself, but also Ada, Walter, Adelé, and Constance. I was even Jean Kraft, whose dream this hotel was in the first place and I felt their spirits stir deep within my cells.

My mother had brought a copy of a small book with her, *From Crown To Crown* and, as she snored peacefully in our hotel room that night, I quietly sneaked it from her suitcase. This was the story of the Kraft family, compiled and written by Pierre Reist, another of my cousins and a great-great-grandson to Jean Kraft. Tucked inside the book was a copy of Constance's eulogy, also translated into English by Pierre.

Mrs. Constance Johanna Maryha
Wieland, née Kraft, daughter of Mr. Jean

281

Kraft and his wife Adelé Rüfenacht; born
May 2, 1840, died December 7, 1920.
....Blessed are the dead who now die in
the Lord, for the spirit talks. May they rest
from their labours and their achievements
follow them.
....Constance Wieland was the second of
seven siblings. From her father she inherited
an iron will. Her mother died giving birth to
the seventh child, and being the oldest
daughter, Constance assumed the role of
surrogate mother at age sixteen. At the same
time she was her father's right hand in the
hotel, active, energetic and competent. She
often had to and wanted to take charge.
When her father married again she found it
difficult to relinquish her role...

Constance met her husband in the
Bernerhof and they'd married in 1861. Together
they'd taken over a hotel in Glarus, a beautiful
alpine town at the foot of Mount Glärnisch
southeast of Zurich. The obituary continued:

...the energetic and circumspect daughter
of her father, the right hand of her husband
and, more yet, the soul of the house, the
collaborator of her husband the first thing in
the morning, the last at night, kind and just
towards employees without neglecting her
duties toward the family. The high point of
this period was the birth of her two
daughters for whom she was mother in the
truest sense of the word.

1868 brought the death of Constance's
father and management of the Bernerhof
transferred to his oldest son Alexander Kraft.

Alexander needed help with the large establishment and recruiting his sister and her husband, they moved back to Berne in 1871.

....In Berne new responsibilities waited for her in the big establishment with the numerous employees and the numerous guests who came and went. There was something royal in her doings and in her ways. She found the correct tone towards noble and simple people, always kind and just, she found time to mother sick employees and to comfort dying waiters. It is here that she endured the heaviest blow of her life, her youngest child, Gustav, was taken from her at the age of nine by an awful sickness.

Her sorrow continued when, in 1897, her daughter, Adelé, became a widow at the age of thirty-five with five young boys to bring up. Constance's husband stepped up and assumed responsibility for the boys, moving them from London back to Berne only to die of a heart attack himself soon after.

....Still, Constance didn't break down. Her new responsibilities revitalized her old energy and will. She wanted to provide a home and be a mother and grandmother all the more. She was there for them all with advice and action, taking care of their schooling and education with motherly love and a positive attitude.

The minister closed the service by saying, "If it was precious, it was hardship, labour and sorrow."

How awesome would it have been to grow up in a grand hotel with an artistic painter for a mother and an accomplished grandmother hanging out with kings and queens?

Joy often comes simply from knowing you are part of something larger than yourself and that you have people on your team—people whose immediate intuition is to love you because of the commonalities you share. What a wonderful gift our ancestors gave us simply by having us. Did they know what joy they were spreading by meeting, marrying, and having children who would go on and do the same through time?

Our last day in Switzerland was spent with my cousin, Barbara, viewing the greening countryside, lunching at a winery, and visiting her home where she lovingly gifted me one of Adelé's artworks: a charcoal drawing of her beloved Sanary that now hangs over my desk.

*What if I had never found my mother? What if I'd never experienced all of this?*

I had just won the gazillion-dollar lottery!

Headed Home

9 May 2008

Our journey half over, with tears in our eyes and sadness in our hearts we said farewell to our Swiss family. The flight from Zurich to Stockholm gave us time to assimilate the events of the week and to relax in preparation for the Swedish portion of the trip.

There, the welcoming scenario was repeated with mother's cousin Anders, his wife Gunilla, my cousins Asa and Ylva and their families (descendants of Walter's brother Arvid).

I found it necessary to keep the European page of our family tree close at hand, referring to it often in order to keep all these people—and my connection to them—straight.

Sweden reminded me of my own Maine coast with its rocky shore covered in tall pines and assorted sailboats dotting the white-capped northern blue waters. Cousin Asa and her family treated us to a picnic of cold cuts, cheeses, salads and assorted breads at their grey weatherworn cottage that faced the glistening waters of the archipelago. A dock held a wood-fired sauna in a small hut, offering a picturesque view to the east, then continued into deeper water where, at its end, their sailboat gently bumped, rocking rhythmically to the symphony of an afternoon breeze. It was a picture perfect setting for a perfect family gathering.

The next day my cousin Ylva hosted us at Gunilla's family home on another coastal shore. Their old many-roomed house was filled to the brim with memorabilia, including several of Adelé's paintings. I found it

285

fascinating that every room held a beautiful tiled stove or fireplace. Tiled stoves were popular in Sweden as they heated quickly and held the heat for a long time. Each stove was unique and the rooms were painted to complement the different colored tiles. In one, a rectangular stove with yellow roses, in another, white with blue ribbons running through it. Several were tucked into the corner of a room saving space and utilizing a central chimney for multiple stoves. My favorite was ornate, round, and cream-colored with little porcelain wine glasses tucked into niches above the stove box with a grand *fleur de lis* crowning the top.

The following day Anders drove while Gunilla narrated a sightseeing tour of Stockholm. The waters surrounding the city reflected majestic, rusty-red brick historical buildings under a clear blue sky. Anders and Gunilla had arranged for my cousins, Maja and Bengt (Walter's brother Gottfrid's grandchildren), to join us for a luncheon cruise. Our lovingly crafted, highly polished wooden riverboat meandered along the river to Drottningholms Slott, the palace residence of Sweden's King since 1981.

Bobbing along, we enjoyed a delightful meal as I intently listened to Maja recount stories of our different family members and of the Lilljeqvist name.

Apparently our family name was originally Gabrielson, son of Gabriel. As our ancestors became more bourgeois, they thought it too common and changed the name to Lilljeqvist after the Lily flower. When Walter and his brother Gustav settled in America, they changed the spelling to Lillieqvist.

Mom had heard all theses stories before and was anxious for the cruise to be over so she could see firsthand the famous Stockholm City Hall, venue for the Nobel Prize Awards. Our family had history there too. Maja explained that Rudolph Lilljeqvist, Walter's brother and good friend of Alfred Nobel, was one of the executors of the coveted prize. *My goodness, what else had this amazing family been involved in?*

After almost two weeks, a longing for the comfort of home surfaced. It had been an overwhelmingly emotional trip and as much as I loved my mother, I longed for some quiet alone time. Morning walks along the river near our hotel gave me some of the solitude I needed to come to grips with the experiences of the past ten days.

Somewhere over the vast Atlantic Ocean, bound for Boston, I put my hand over Ada's, "Mom, I know it wasn't easy for you physically or financially to take this trip. It's meant a lot to me. Thanks for doing this. I love you."

"I love you too, Carol Ann," she said, fuchsia lips stretching ear to ear. "I'm glad we did this together. You've met a lot of family. I hope you'll keep in touch with them over the years. Family's important!"

The trip was such a special blessing. No one treated me like the unwanted guest who shows up uninvited on the doorstep, or the embarrassing member of the family everyone wishes was in someone else's family rather than theirs.

"But you know, Carol Ann, what has healed me the most has been the telling. It's the telling of our story that has freed me of the shame of my secret."

Sitting in silence holding her hand, I too thought about how telling my story to people I loved and trusted had freed me, how writing this book has opened parts of me I didn't even know needed freeing.

Nodding, cheeks rising to meet my eyes in a smile, I said, "Knowing my biological roots—who I came from is so important. Now I can be who I really am."

Ada wiped at tears, hugging me tightly, then sniffled. Placing my younger hand over her delicate arthritic wrist, I felt her pulse gradually slow, her hand become limp as she drifted off to sleep.

How fortunate I was! I shared my ancestors' gifts of creativity, humor, and positive attitude that gave us the ability to survive in the face of adversity; most importantly we shared a resolve to story our own life, instead of allowing someone else to do that for us.

My life would have been different if my mother had kept and raised me all those years ago. Certainly, our strong wills would have clashed often in heated arguments, but it would have been a life filled with love, laughter, and family.

I'd probably have liked growing up in Kansas on a farm, driving the tractor, shoveling manure, spreading seed, harvesting my labors, and sitting around a fire or on the front porch with family, perhaps even siblings. I might not have traveled or known as much of the world as I do. It certainly would have been different—not better or worse, just different.

Alone with my thoughts, yet never less lonely, I reflected on the long process of becoming whole, squaring with my past, making things right, nailing myself down. Proud of myself for meeting life's challenges head-on, a deep gratitude spread from my core in waves like a single drop of water falling into a pond radiating energetic rings outward.

Here I was again, at a place of new beginnings—an adult adolescence—redefining identity—only this time with open eyes and a better understanding of myself, softening, becoming less rough around the edges, less driven. Oh, the fire within still burns brightly—but with fewer flare-ups.

Epilogue

Gazing out over the purple mountain majesty of Western Maine's Mahoosic Mountain Range with New Hampshire's Mount Washington's Cool-Whip® peaks contrasting the red, yellow, and russet of fall leaves, Indian summer sunshine bolts through holes in the pewter clouds like tiny flashlights, illuminating the earth in a gloaming glow that casts cone-shaped shadows from the fir trees onto our yard. Closing my eyes, I open my hands with palms upward, resting them comfortably on my lap, and allow my physical body to pool into the warm chair as my mind becomes blank.

With a rib-expanding breath, I conjure up my Dream Woman.

*"Constance, I wish I'd been able to give my children a larger sense of family while they were growing up, but how do you do that if you haven't experienced that yourself?*

*"How can I best help Laura? Will she know if or when it's right for her to seek her birth family? Will her mother greet her with open arms as Ada did me—or deal her a crushing blow of rejection?*

*"What twists and turns will John V face over his lifetime— will I know the right things to do or say in support?*

*"Does my first son know he's adopted? What might he need or want from me? Will I be able to give it, if he asks? Will there come a day when he sees an old faded photograph and squares with himself?"*

Dear Reader,

My hope is that my story will have entertained, as well as, inspired you. Dream your dreams. Reach for your own stars and believe in the truth that you can walk your own path rising above whatever adversity comes your way.

A graphic of a braided circle with a square gem appears throughout the book and completes a full circle itself.

In a circle all is equal: no one is ahead or behind, above or below, better or less than any other.

The strands represent the birth family or birthmother, the adoptee, and the adopted family or adoptive parent. These strands intertwine signifying the influence each has on the other.

The square gem exemplifies adoptees coming to a place of solidarity within themselves over their dual identity.

This braided circular symbol has become my logo along with inspiring a new line of custom-made jewelry specifically designed for those touched by foster care and adoption.

If you would like to share your own story with me, or are interested in learning more about my Adoption Jewelry, I invite you to visit my website http://www.carol-welsh.com/, email me at carol@carol_welsh.com, or like me on Facebook at: https://www.facebook.com/pages/360-Square-by-Carol-L-Welsh/102249556556534

I look forward to hearing from you.
Carol

# Acknowledgements

It takes a lifetime of experience, encouragement, serendipity, and preparation to bring a book to publication. Without the help of many people this book would still be mulling around in my mind.

The first person I want to thank is Ada May Lillieqvist, for it was she who gave me life, genes, and unconditional love.

Next I am grateful to all my adoptive families, for through them I learned strength and how to deal with adversity, as well as how to love and appreciate all that I have.

After that, I'm forever grateful to everyone who has woven his or her way through my life.

I want to thank my family and friends for the overwhelming support and encouragement they so willingly offered. I particularly appreciate the help of Carol R., Libby S., Shannon S., and Kathy H. for brainstorming, reading, feedback, insights, and re-reading and formatting help they have selflessly provided over many hours.

I'm also indebted to all my colleagues at work, especially Alison and Jeanne, who have patiently tolerated my incessant discussions about "the book."

To all the professional people—Kerry, Susan, Christine, Lisa, Cory, Susan, Judy and Kate who have helped with edits, proof reading, marketing, web design, and just being there when I needed you, as well as Josh at The Maine Writers and Publisher Alliance and my fellow writers and authors, I gratefully say, "You're the best."

Of course, this book wouldn't have happened without the enthusiastic support of my partner, Dick, who has never once complained about me turning our small comfortable living room into a messy office.

Lastly, I want to acknowledge my Dream Woman, for without her comfort and guidance my path would definitely have been darker.

# About the Author

Carol Ann Lillieqvist Welsh lives life with passion. Even her astrologer says she's, "just too much!"

Carol holds a bachelor's degree in Psychology, a master's in Human Relations, and is a Registered Nurse, educator, and business owner. She is a member of the Maine Writers and Publishers Alliance, the American Adoption Congress, and the Association of Camp Nurses.

Her desire is to offer a unique understanding of adoption from the perspective of one person who has experienced all sides of the triad. She hopes to inspire others to set goals, trusting in their ability to make dreams come true. She encourages people to color outside the lines, be true to themselves, and take part in their own destinies through her example.

She currently works as a nurse in obstetrics at Stephens Memorial Hospital in western Maine. Since 2002, Carol has also attended to the medical needs of staff and campers at Camp Wigwam, a residential boys camp, in Maine. Each August she also makes time to provide nursing coverage for Camp To Belong Maine®, an organization that provides opportunity for Maine siblings, separated by foster care and adoption, to re-unite in a safe and supervised environment.

An avid traveler, Carol is always up for a new adventure. She lives in Norway, Maine with Dick and spends time with her children and grandchildren as often as possible.